To my mom, my three heartbeats and my love

To my sisters, brothers and to the brokenhearted

GRACE FOR THE JOURNEY

Published by
Watersprings Media House
7095 Hacks Cross Road, #129
Olive Branch, MS 38654
www.waterspringsmedia.com
Contact publisher for bulk orders and permission requests.

Copyright © 2015 by Athena C. Shack

All rights reserved. No part of this publication may be reproduced, distributed, or transmitted in any form or by any means, including photocopying, recording, or other electronic or mechanical methods, without the prior written permission of the publisher, except in the case of brief quotations embodied in critical reviews and certain other noncommercial uses permitted by copyright law.

Printed in the United States of America

ISBN-10: 0692512179
ISBN-13: 978-0-692-51217-3
Library of Congress Control Number: 2015914721

Scripture quotations taken from The Holy Bible, New International Version® NIV® Copyright © 1973, 1978, 2011 by Biblica, Inc. ™ Used by permission. All rights reserved worldwide.

Scripture quotations taken from The Holy Bible, New King James Version © 1982 by Thomas Nelson, Inc. All rights reserved. Used by permission.

The Scripture quotations contained herein are from the New Revised Standard Version Bible, copyright © 1989, Division of Christian Education of the National Council of Churches in Christ in the U.S.A. Used by permission. All rights reserved.

Cover design: Watersprings Media House
Background image © Robertsrob/123rf.com

Grace for the Journey

Navigating back to the land of the living after tragedy, trauma or loss.

Athena C. Shack

CONTENTS

FOREWORD

SECTION ONE: *Your Place*

1. That Place Called There — 11
2. Defeating Weapons of Mass Torture — 25
3. Grace in the Shadow of Death — 45

SECTION TWO: *Your Journey*

4. Navigating Destiny Detours — 61
5. The Road to Your Comeback — 73
6. Living on Hope Until Help Arrives — 85

SECTION THREE: *Your New Life*

7. Reservations in Your New Season — 97
8. New Purpose on the Other Side of Pain — 111
9. The Victory Lap — 123

FOREWORD

For only God, in Divine ability, wisdom and providence is able to position our lives like pieces in a Chess Game and achieve grace-laced results no matter the circumstances and all without asking our permission. Our God is truly amazing! Amazing not just because this book is being released but amazing because of the journey that it took to get here. I am excited to commend all that read this book.

As stated, God will position and reposition us by the sheer power and insight of the Lord's will. This will happen often without our permission and will even some, if not most time include tragedy, trauma or loss. This is why the Lord cannot trust us to write our own stories because we would leave out the painful episodes and excruciating chapters. We would leave out the cancer, the death of a loved one, the disease or dis-ease, and that heartbreak or heartache. That is why this book is so refreshing.

Minister Shack speaks to and is a testimony to the fact that whether you know it or not God is always at work even when there is no evidence present. She reminds us that the Lord's heart for us can always be trusted even when God's hand in our lives seemingly cannot be traced. It is when this is realized that we can be assured that processes in life might be hard but they're fair because our Sovereign God provides grace for the journey. Enjoy!

Dr. Eugene L. Gibson Jr.,

Senior Pastor, Olivet Fellowship Church, Memphis, TN,
Author of *Courage Under Fire*

Psalm 116:1-9 (NIV)

¹ I love the Lord, for he heard my voice;
he heard my cry for mercy.
² Because he turned his ear to me,
I will call on him as long as I live.

³ The cords of death entangled me,
the anguish of the grave came over me;
I was overcome by distress and sorrow.
⁴ Then I called on the name of the Lord:
"Lord, save me!"

⁵ The Lord is gracious and righteous;
our God is full of compassion.
⁶ The Lord protects the unwary;
when I was brought low, he saved me.

⁷ Return to your rest, my soul,
for the Lord has been good to you.

⁸ For you, Lord, have delivered me from death,
my eyes from tears,
my feet from stumbling,
⁹ that I may walk before the Lord
in the land of the living.

SECTION ONE

Your Place

1

That Place Called There

"Save me, O God, for the waters have come up to my neck. I sink in the miry depths, where there is no foothold. I have come into the deep waters; the floods engulf me. I am worn out calling for help; my throat is parched. My eyes fail, looking for my God."

Psalm 69:1-3 (NIV)

As long as I can remember, I have held a passport and traveled quite often as a child. My favorite places to travel are locations with beautiful, sandy beaches and crystal blue waters. I love the idea of going to new countries and experiencing other cultures. Simply planning the trip is exciting and the anticipation of a great vacation builds with each new adventure on the itinerary. When we travel, we not only hope, but expect sunny skies, great weather and calm seas. Even though, we know that the weather is uncontrollable and sometimes unpredictable. Wind and rain can hurl down unexpectedly on anyone, at any time, and in any place. Then we have to adjust our itinerary, manage our disappointment and develop new plans. Isn't that just like life? It is just as uncontrollable and unpredictable as the weather.

Sometimes, we treat our lives like a well-planned vacation expecting only sunny skies and undeterred plans. Unfortunately, life isn't that controllable. As a matter of fact, at any given time our plans can be altered by an unforeseen event, tragedy or traumatic experience. Not only will your life plans have to change, but the act of navigating through that place is painful and often unbearable. Times such as these will usher you into an unexpected and unwanted place.

Perhaps you know this place to which I am referring. It is that place that you never visited before and didn't know much about. It is a place you often wished could be erased from the passport of your life. In that place, there aren't any fragrant and beautiful flowers to adorn your neck when you arrive. A concierge is not available to address your accommodation concerns. You do not even receive a welcome brochure detailing the daily activities and excursion highlights. The most frustrating part of this place is that you do not have the opportunity to make the reservations nor approve the itinerary. All you know is that one day it was sunny, clear skies and warm temperatures, and the next day, you are "There." If events in your life have ushered you to that place called There, you are not alone.

Stranger in the Land

Naomi, Ruth's mother-in-law in the book of Ruth, also found herself in that place called There. She was married with two sons and lived in Judah until a famine caused them to relocate to Moab. During early times, for a woman to be married and bear children it was the equivalent to being wealthy. The social status of a woman was at the bottom of the barrel next to the poor. Widows, orphans and immigrants were placed alongside the poor, but in many occasions would be treated as less than them. Women did not even have the same opportunities as the average, poor, adult male Israelite. In this patriarchal social structure, widows were dependent on their fathers, husbands or in the absence of both, the obedience and kindness of others.

Consequently, manpower was needed for sustenance and usually the male was that source of provision as well as the covering. Without the male, the woman was left extremely vulnerable. Having children in this culture was imperative to carry on the family lineage and in most cases to contribute to the family's economic stability.

Therefore, being married with children, led to a stable 'happily ever after life.' Presumably, Naomi was living that life until the time of the famine. Ruth chapter one records, that while in Moab, her husband died. Naomi and her two sons lived in Moab for ten years, took wives for themselves, and then they both died there as well. Now, Naomi was a widow, childless and a stranger in the land.

When I relocated from the North to the South, the most frequently asked question I was asked was "How in the world did you get from New York to Mississippi?" Everyone wanted to know why I would leave the big city and move to a small town in Mississippi. I was asked if I had family there or if my job relocated me? For a long time I evaded those questions because I did not know how to answer from an honest place without revealing the painful reality of my journey.

The reality was that New York was not my home; I was born and raised in Connecticut. New York was the place I went to so that I could live out my dreams. It was the place I obtained my college education. It was the place where I got married, had my first child and bought my first house. It was the place that I stayed for 18 years and had the life that I wanted until it was all gone.

It was now the place that my husband died, I became a widow at 35, single mother looking at foreclosure and receiving food stamps. It was the place where I found myself There. There, is the place where you never expected to be. It is the place where you are suddenly drowning in a sea of despair and tidal waves of hopelessness crashes into your prayers and faith. There, is a place of darkness. There, is a place of brokenness. There, is a place of pain and grief. Instead of white sandy beaches, cliffs and valleys fill the landscape. Instead of light blue skies, darkness and muddy slopes create a new horizon. No one wants to be There, but unfortunately, some of us will either visit or become an involuntary resident, like myself, Naomi and countless others.

The question is, how do you leave an unfamiliar and dark place when you can't see yourself out? How do you get back to the sunny life in the land of the living when you are lost in the thicket of despair and uncertainty? Typical maps and navigational systems are useless in finding your location and providing directions out. The event, the tragedy, the trauma or the loss left you in an unknown territory; however, you are expected to find your way back to life. If that is not bad enough, you also do not know how long you will be There. What was the tragic event that caused the trauma or loss in your life that has brought you to that place called There?

The Event

- Abuse
- Accident
- Addiction
- Adultery
- Amputation
- Cancer
- Death(s)
- Divorce
- Flood
- Hurricane
- Illness
- Incest
- Kidnapping
- Miscarriage(s)
- Murder
- Prison
- Rape(s)
- Sexual Assault
- Stillborn
- Suicide
- Tornado
- War

Everyone may have a different "it," a different story preceded by a different event but the pain of the circumstances puts us in the same place. In your story, there is probably a climatic event, a major moment of impact, a shock and a horror that takes place. You can recount the moment you heard the news or recall each detail as it happened to you personally and all the emotions it brought to the forefront.

Tragic stories are always delivered by surprise, aren't they? The event(s) that led you to that place was not proceeded by an email, certified letter, telephone call or text; although advance notice wouldn't make much difference in the story. The reality is whether we expected it or not, it happened and it hurt.

I was living the old "American dream" until the one fateful day I awoke to a horror. I was married to a gorgeous law enforcement officer, with a rambunctious three and half year old son, living in a nice house, in a great neighborhood and busy in God's business. In the church, I was a teacher, the church administrator, and trustee and just serving the body of Christ and the leadership in whatever capacity I was gifted to do so. However, the next day my entire world changed when I became a part of a murder-suicide attempt, and entered that place called There.

It was 7:52 a.m. when the course of my life changed forever. It was at that moment I decided to go upstairs from the basement after having slept there all night after an intense discussion with my husband. I walked up the stairs of my bi-level home with no plan of action or to even engage my husband in any more dialogue because we had hit a communication wall.

As I began to walk down our hall toward the bedrooms, I saw him fully dressed walking towards me. I started to ask where he was going, but all I could get out was "wh" before he extended his arm around my neck. He dragged me backwards by my throat down the hall onto the dining room floor.

My wonderful husband, who was well respected and loved by everyone, woke up that morning with the intention to kill me, and then him. The spirits of guilt and shame had convinced my husband that he didn't deserve to live, and that there was no way to escape the pain and shame that he had caused me, and his family. My husband had been carrying a secret, a marital infidelity, which resulted in a child. This haunted him for months, maybe even a year and apparently I stumbled across this truth, which became the cause of his demise.

The Trauma

I laid on the floor with a 255 lb., 6'1" man on top of my petite, with one arm wrapped around my neck and the other wrapped around my waist attempting to literally squeeze the life out of me. At one point, I thought I was bleeding internally when it felt as if my organs were being squeezed and moved out of the way to give place to his bulging biceps.

My spiritual survival instincts sprung into action and I started to say "Jesus," repeatedly until the air was gone from my tiny wind pipes. Time moved so slowly that I became deaf to the usual white noise of my home. The humming refrigerator faded, the chirping birds quieted and the baseboard radiators were silenced. My senses began to numb one at a time but I had an internal megaphone that didn't fail even when my vocal chords did.

While struggling to breathe and waiting to die, at that moment I realized that everything I was, and everything that I had attained meant nothing. As I waited to pass out from asphyxiation, I glared at the kitchen cabinets on the floor as the sun from the window hit them with its rays. Then it happened. My life began to flash before my eyes. However, unlike many others who have near death experiences, it wasn't my past that flashed before me, it was my future. I began to recall everything that God said to me regarding my life.

When I was in my twenties, in prayer, God told me that I would write a book. God showed me auditoriums and seats to the places I would be speaking. How could this then be happening to me? I did not get the opportunity to fulfill God's plans for my life. Now, I was facing what I believed to be certain death. There was no way out for me. I literally could not move or speak. I just waited for the extension in his arm that was slowly pulling my neck up to the ceiling to finally pop my neck. When that angle did not appear to work, he slowly turned my neck to the side in an effort to snap it from that direction.

At that moment, all I could do was ponder what the newspapers and TV news would report. At that time, I did not know why this was happening to me and was embarrassed at how my story was going to end. I was lying on the floor in my teal nightgown being strangled by my loving husband of nine years and friend of 17 years. I couldn't believe it and I didn't understand it. I was about to become a news report and a statistic and I didn't understand why. How did I arrive to that place called There?

Television and media has often been accused of desensitizing our emotions. Tragic events are made into television miniseries, cinematic movies and re-depicted in documentaries. However, it is these events that have shattered lives and propelled people into a perpetual state of crisis.

Trauma can be described as the response to any event that shatters our safe world. Trauma leaves a person feeling unsafe in a place that used to be safe. The American Psychological Association defines trauma as "an emotional response to a terrible event like an accident, rape or natural disaster. Immediately after the event, shock and denial are typical. Longer term reactions include unpredictable emotions, flashbacks, strained relationships and even physical symptoms like headaches or nausea. While these feelings are normal, some people have difficulty moving on with their lives.[1] Christians are not excluded from tragedy, trauma and loss. Just think about the stories of loss and tragedy for Adam and Eve, Job, David, Naomi and Mary, the mother of Jesus.

When you can't fight physically, make the choice to fight spiritually.

The Tragedy. The Loss.

When my one and only child walked in the room and saw his loving father strangling mommy, I knew I had to fight for my life for my son's sake. My husband loved his son and when he yelled at him to go back to his room, it was out of love. My son, as young and scared as he was, was smart enough to bring me my cell phone when he heard it ringing. I used that opportunity to physically fight more and gain control of my vocals to plead with my husband whose mind at that time was completely under the influence of demonic spirits. I repeatedly told him, *"I love you. I love you. I love you."* I told him that our son needed us, and that he could not do this. He had a quick retort and I was shocked he had such a ready reply. It allowed me to see his love for his son but at the same time the depths of his fears of me, and his family living through the pain of his secret.

The more I struggled with him physically, he began speaking and I finally heard the distress in his voice and saw the panic and snare in his eyes. In all the years that I have known him, I had never seen his eyes glare in that manner. They were red, dazed and unfocused. At first, I tried reasoning with him, but my husband of 9 years and friend of 17 years, was no longer there mentally or spiritually. So, I had to switch survival strategies and talk directly to that spirit that was trying to take my life, abort my purpose and make an orphan out of my son.

I began to bind up the spirit of murder. I chose to fight spiritually when I could not fight physically. You can be in the most powerless position in life but that does not negate the power of God that lives in you.

As a law enforcement officer, he was trained in hand-to-hand combat, and had the strength and opportunity to break my neck and he tried. But it was the love of God and his own love for me that kept his arms from taking my life that day.

As hard as it is to believe, I never once felt anger from him. I was not dealing with an angry nor aggressive spirit. His arms wrapped around my body tightly but I felt as if he was holding on to me and un-wanting to let me go as a husband un-wanting to let go of his bride. I felt the love in his arms, and that love conquered my death that day. My husband loved me too much to kill me and take away his son's mother. His last words to me that day were, "Athena, I loved you. I loved you. I always loved you. Take care of our son. Everything that you need, all the papers are in the drawer. I love you."

My husband fled from our house that day and jumped off a bridge to his death leaving me a widow at 35 and my son fatherless at 3 ½. His body wasn't recovered for several weeks from the freezing waters of winter. During that time of uncertainty, fear, and uttermost pain, I had to either sink or swim myself. Every day that came and went, I felt like I was drowning in the sea of despair of my broken life. Everything I knew, and everything I had was gone. I was in that place called There, involuntarily and with no departure in sight.

However, my life was not over and I was soon about to discover that God was just getting started with me. A part of me was going to die, but it was not going to be the death I expected. God was not about to let me die with the purpose that was within me. I am more valuable to Him alive. My life as well as my son's life and purpose were destined to come to fruition. My husband's life and death were a part of that destiny.

The Journey

While this is my personal story, you have your own individual passport stamped with personal trails of abuse, traumatic experiences, tragedy, death, loss or betrayal. There comes a moment in each of your lives where you are faced with that situation, that place, that trial of your faith that was designed to prove you, make you or break you.

Yet, it is the darkest and lowest place you have ever been in your life and you feel hopeless and powerless. Your breaths quicken. Your mind wanders uncontrollably. You can be in a room full of people and feel all alone, isolated and drowning in your thoughts of what just happened. Tragedy struck your life and landed you in the unknown, unchartered, scary place called There. The murder, the car accident, the suicide, the kidnapping, the sexual abuse, the bombing, the shooting, the war, the divorce, the diagnosis – it landed you There.

If you are able to relate to that place, the place that I call There, then you know there is no cliché, snappy phrase or quick fix to get you out of that place. There is not a single scripture to read that will make everything all right. A "church shout" and "speak it and claim it" falls short of anything more than hot air. The reality is that it will be an arduous journey from that place to a place of healing, restoration and new life.

This is probably the most painful journey you will embark on in your life. You will need to develop a new skill set designed for a place like this. You may want to run away but no place seems safe. You may want to hide but no place seems far enough. You may want to talk but no one seems to understand. It will take a combination of things to get you through it.

In this book, my prayer is that you develop and sharpen your survival skill set while discovering more about your divine purpose and God along the way. Consider me your tour guide that provides instruction, shares experiences and gives encouragement for that journey. Each chapter will close with C.A.P.S: confession, application, prayer starters and scripture meditation. These are practical action steps designed to empower you each step of the way as you navigate back to the land of the living.

❧ Journey Steps ❧

❧ *Confession:* In spite of my place of _____ (name your situation) I shall not die in there but I will be healed, I will be made whole and I shall live the abundant life God has prepared for me.

❧ *Application:* As painful as it is, recall your event and write down every emotion connected with it. When you begin to feel these emotions overtaking your daily thoughts, read a Psalm and write down which Psalm speaks to your heart condition and pray through it.

❧ *Prayer Starter:* Dear God, I cry out to you in the midst of this place of distress. I yield to you every emotion, hurt, disappointment and pain. God, reveal to me your will for my life that I may grasp hold to it and never lose sight of it. Allow me to put this event in my life into the full context of your plan for my life. Breathe your breath of life on me again so that I may live. Steady my feet for this journey, and be a light to my path.

❧ *Scripture Meditation:* Psalm 116

2

Defeating Weapons of Mass Torture

"For our weapons of our warfare are not merely human, but they have divine power to destroy strongholds"

2 Corinthians 10:4 (NRSV)

One day a friend of mine and I were driving to the airport. I saw a woman stumbling across the street as we waited for the light to turn green. He recognized her as a fixture in the community and began to tell me her story. She was an Ivy League, educated woman who had a bustling career and was happily married. When her husband was murdered in front of her, she never recovered from the tragedy. She ended up a victim of drug abuse, prostitution and HIV. Although, I had never met her and only heard of her story, I sympathized with her.

It is not unheard of for people who experience horrific tragedies or traumas to end up in psychiatric wards and eventually living off of prescription drugs. Emotional roller coasters can render you dizzy and confused. They cause you to feel as if you are losing your mind. Often during grief counseling, the first thing people admit to, is feeling like they are "losing their mind," or "going crazy." This is often what leads them to seek counseling. That young lady's story easily could have been my story. In the aftermath of her personal tragedy, she found herself "There" and had simply lost her mind and could not renew it. She was defeated by the trauma, the tragedy and did not recover from what she lost.

During a time of tragedy, trauma or loss, the enemy of your soul will take advantage of that season and will launch a less than subtle attack against your spirit. Weapons of mass torture are designed to exaggerate your emotional state and annihilate your God given purpose. If you are not careful, these weapons can force you to live in a false reality of a never ending pain and a life God did not intend for you. You have to realize that the weapons you are being attacked with are not sent from God to wound us any further. That is not the kind of God we serve. If we are being honest with ourselves we would admit that we blame God on some level for allowing horrific things to happen to us or people that we love.

Unfortunately, many people turn their backs on God during this time and will begin to believe the negative, inner voices that God doesn't care or God is punishing them. That is exactly the kind of thinking that the enemy of our soul feeds into and perpetuates through spiritual attacks and consistent torture.

Weapons of mass torture are designed to pour salt in an open wound and exacerbate our pain. Its infrastructure is created to distract and derail you from the purpose and plan that God has for your life. If the enemy can cause you to feel increased pain it will send you further into a pit of hopelessness and create faithlessness. It can even cause you to become bitter and angry with people and with God. Often people will end up in depression, not by the initial hurt or event but with what tortures them daily.

The Assassin's Weapons

Grief, sorrow and pain deliver many things during your darkest days. In one of my days, I was caught off guard by what I can only describe as the intense presence of the Lord that engulfed my home. The atmosphere was so full of God's divine presence that all I could do was bow down and worship God. My worship led me to a prostrate position on my dining room floor. As I worshipped God, I heard a voice in my spirit that said, *"Look up."* I sat up and then looked toward the ceiling adorned with a chandelier that my late husband installed. The black metal chandelier began to fade and what I saw next amazed me to my feet. I stood slowly and glared at the large artillery weapons I saw suspended in mid-air. I was surrounded by numerous large, machine guns and rifles fully loaded and aimed. I slowly turned 360 degrees, pointing at each weapon in amazement as if I could identify each by name.

This could have been a terrifying sight for me, but fear did not make its approach because I was in the presence of God. Instead, I was comforted by the vision. It was the most dramatic and vivid vision I had ever received to date. It reminded me that the weapons were formed, armed and even aimed, but they could not kill me. That was comforting. However, I would soon come to experience that what doesn't kill me, could still torture me. Life events can easily bring you into a spiritual battle after tragedy, trauma or loss.

The night my husband committed suicide, I will never forget the rain, which maliciously fell down to the ground beating on my house as a reminder that my husband's body was outside in a watery grave. It rained long and it rained hard. The melody of this rain was not soothing or peaceful as the trained element of water gently refreshes the earth. No, it rained long and it rained hard. It was a mean downpour that night. It had no remorse. It had no sympathy. Visions of angry rain-water pushing my husband's body through a helpless current of the usually calm river tormented me as I lay in the bed trying to sleep. I became angry at the rain and I felt that as long as it rained the further it would push his body from me. The rain became my new enemy but not my only one. When you are in that place called There, you will find yourself in a spiritual battle against many things, often simple things.

During a time of mourning, friends and family will say to you, *"You need to get some rest."* They mean well and by all means that is reasonable counsel. To the grieving or hurting person whose world just collapsed, nothing that they did the day before and the thousands of days before that seems normal, including sleep. Sleep is not enjoyable. Sleep is for those who are at peace. Sleep is for the other people whose minds are not wandering thinking about every last minute and detail of the event that robbed them of their normal life. Who would have thought, that even sleep could be a form of torture.

On the other hand, sleep is sometimes an escape. I thought, if I can just go to sleep, my mind will just shut down all the thoughts and numb the pain for those few hours. Unfortunately, due to the tragic circumstances surrounding my husband's death, sleep became a quiet time of torture for me. When those around me thought I was resting or getting a good night's sleep, there was nothing good or restful about it. For months, I had nightmares of my husband returning to our home from his watery grave trying to get into our house. He appeared at various doors and entrances trying to gain entrance, never once saying a word or showing any signs of anger. I saw images of my dead spouse dressed in the clothes he left in just wanting to come home.

Every single one of those dreams petrified me and created a paradox for me at the same time. Although, I knew he was dead, as his loving wife of 9 years, I longed for him to be alive but was traumatized by his attempt on my life and yet still grieved his death. My heart was conflicted with my fears. My fears were conflicted with my heart. And, my love for him became an enemy to our last embrace. It was the worst kind of torture imaginable and I waited anxiously for the dawn of a new day and every day thereafter. I no longer awoke each day to the quiet suburban neighborhood that I lived in. No. I awoke to and lived in the dark, cold shadow of death that tortured my soul daily. What tortures your heart and soul? Is it a memory? A scent? A visual? A touch? A sound? A dream?

The spirit of recall is very busy after horrific events. You will replay events and conversations over and over uncontrollably. Traumatic events will begin to affect how you see yourself. You could be the most confident, rational, faithful person before the event. After the event, you are overwhelmed, lack confidence, feel unstable, angry and have the privilege of daily re-experiencing the trauma mentally. The enemy of your soul will use those thoughts to torture you into unrest. An unrest that people around you don't seem to understand causing you to feel isolated with your thoughts, emotions and tortured soul.

Left Alone to Fight

When people have not experienced what you have experienced they cannot empathize with you. This is frustrating for not only you but also for your friends and family who feel helpless to help you. I know my family and friends were not able to understand how difficult my mourning process was. I didn't have to contend with just a death.

I had a husband who I loved, who tried to kill me, committed suicide because he couldn't face living with the consequences of an infidelity that resulted in a child. I didn't know what to grieve first. I was overwhelmed with horrific thoughts, fears, emotions and sorrow. My marriage was over. My son was fatherless. I lost hope for the future of having more children or even finding a husband who would want to be married to a woman whose husband killed himself. I didn't have a sense of security because the attack rendered me suspicious of people in close quarters with me. When I went outside the house, I was constantly looking over my shoulder in fear of him returning to finish what he started thanks to the weapons of mass torture. During the course of my day, I also feared running into anyone I knew because I didn't want them to ask me questions about his death.

If people could look into your fears right now, what would they see? Would they understand? Often times we just want somebody to say I understand what you are going through and mean it. Does it take away the pain? Definitely not, however it provides a glimmer of hope that you are not alone and you can make it too. Unfortunately, sometimes you may be left alone to fight. You may find it hard finding a support group, blog or Facebook group for your particular situation. There are times when well-meaning friends and family members become "miserable comforters" making the situation even harder. Counseling and therapy are typically good options for those struggling with these issues, however, many people stray away from these resources for many reasons. Or in my case, the counseling attempts just weren't sufficient for my circumstances.

Understandably, my late husband's family didn't know how to cope with such a wild course of events from the brother and son whom they knew for over 40 years. The church members, which consisted of all my friends and were considered my family, were told not to contact me in an effort to respect my privacy. Initially, that seemed like sound advice coming from the church leaders, but it ended up being the worst possible thing for the person who had now felt completely abandoned by her husband, his family and now everyone else that I thought cared for me.

There were a few that didn't follow the church's command and called me regardless. Years later, it still means so much to me to know that somebody cared enough about me to pick up the phone, hear my voice and let me know that they cared. They didn't ask questions, but yielded themselves for whatever I needed. Sadly, all I needed was a genuine hug. For weeks and months, I yearned for someone to just wrap their arms around me and hug me until I released the bowels of tears and emotions that couldn't be articulated in words. All I wanted was just a hug.

I learned during that experience that as a Church, we do not truly know how to care for the wounded. I highly recommend a book by H. Norman Wright, *Helping Those Who Hurt*. It helps us to understand those around us that are hurting and avoid contributing to that hurt with clichés and improper responses.

When words can't comfort, a simple gesture or a caring presence can fill the heart of someone that is hurting. Often times we assume people are getting their needs met from those that are closest to them. That is not always the case; just ask Job whose wife and friends were of no substantial help to him during his tragedy. Sometimes the ones that are the closest offer no support because they don't know how or, they are hurting as well. Consequently, we are left alone to dwell in the shadow of our pain, darkness or sorrow.

Tragedy Tortures Your Theology

When tragedy takes place in our lives we are consumed with questions, what-ifs, anger and disbelief. We find ourselves on the other side of happiness and in a seemingly unfair war waged against our souls. I was tortured by the rain, dreams, silence of friends and family, my husband's car, water, a bridge, financial distress, winter's cold temperatures and the never-ending stigma of suicide. You may be tortured by the car accident, miscarriage, divorce, domestic assaults, your sexuality, the infidelity or your unfilled dreams. The enemy of our soul will use these circumstances to wage war on our spirituality, theology, mind, faith, hopes and dreams. We are not all going to experience the same trials in life, but all hurts.

Not only are your emotions, memory and heart tortured during this time, but also your theology. When a 27 year old woman who is 7 months pregnant finds out she has a large, stage four, cancerous tumor pressing on her lungs you begin to question the heart of God. When thousands of people including women and children are swept away in the torrents of a hurricane, you begin to question the authority of God. Tragedy, trauma and loss can torture your theology and your faith in God.

The reality that the death of my husband was caused by suicide devastated my Christian beliefs. I was taught from an early church education that those who committed suicide were sent directly to hell. They do not pass go, nor collect bail. They go straight to hell. This was the very first dagger to my heart when I learned of his death. The image of my husband, who loved God, believed in Jesus as his Lord and Savior yet burning in hell was unbearable and unbelievable. I had to wrestle with what I was taught and what I knew personally about God. I learned a few things that settled my spirit and that could no longer be a source of torture.

First, I did my own personal bible study, and saw that each suicide that was recorded in the bible did not pronounce any judgment of hell on those that committed it. Furthermore, those who receive hell as a judgment is because they have denied Jesus as being the Son of God and their personal Savior. Finally, no one knows the heart condition and the timing of the actual death and repentance can take place before their final demise.

However, only one thing truly convinced me of my husband's final resting place and that was the character of God. I knew God. I have observed the character of God and God's ways. God knew the heart of my husband and although he was not a perfect man, he was still covered and under the blood of Jesus. I have no hesitation in telling my son, that his father is in heaven with God.

In spite of what you are going through, you will have to do some work as you move toward your healing during this journey. You will not be able to just sit and wait for time to pass for you to just feel better. You will need to see and arrest the things in the spirit that are targeting your faith, your purpose and your destiny.

Don't let the enemy use what you see,
to forget what you know.

Cleaning Your Wounds

Guns are the most frequently used weapons of choice in committing murders. According to forensic experts, gunshot wounds can be either *penetrating* or *perforating*. In a penetrating wound, the bullet enters the body and remains inside. In a perforating wound, the bullet passes completely through the body. When a bullet penetrates the skin, it must have an exit. If the bullet stays in the human body, depending on the type of bullet it can explode, poison the body or cause a life threatening infection. The bullet may not kill immediately upon impact, but if it remains inside it tortures the body's immune system.

In order for healing to take place, you need to identify the true source of your pain and uproot it from your mind, and spirit. I learned that when good memories saddened me it was a form of torture and a spiritual attack. Once the good memories lead to the joy it was intended to create, it was my sign that healing had begun. Two of the weapons of mass torture that the enemy used against the children of Israel were fear and doubt, which led them into a 40-year pattern of distress while being tortured with memories.

After the dramatic escape following all the plagues, Pharaoh released them to leave Egypt under the direction of Moses, the deliverer. Then God hardened his heart and he and six hundred chariots and all the chariots of Egypt with captains pursued after them. God wanted everyone to know who God was and would give the children of Israel a miraculous victory by withdrawing the walls of the Red Sea for them to walk across. When the children of Israel saw Pharaoh in pursuit of them, they became very afraid and cried out to God for help, but spoke doubt to Moses.

"They said to Moses, "Was it because there were no graves in Egypt that you brought us to the desert to die?

What have you done to us by bringing us out of Egypt? Didn't we say to you in Egypt, 'Leave us alone; let us serve the Egyptians?' It would have been better for us to serve the Egyptians than to die in the desert!"

Exodus 14:11-12 (NIV)

Just seeing the Egyptians after them caused such fear and intimidation that they would have rather stayed in slavery to the them. They were on the brink of being freed and on their way to the liberty that God promised them. However, when they saw their enemies at their backs they seemed to have forgotten all of the wonders God had performed on their behalf. If we are not careful, the enemy will use what we *see* to forget what we *know*.

The weapons of fear and intimidation will keep you enslaved and thinking that there is no greener pasture, there is no new life after losing a loved one, and there is no better man than the abusive one that you had. During the divorce, he will have you thinking that all men are cheaters and no one can love you like you want to be loved. When we feel at our loneliest and disconnected from friends, family and society the enemy will magnify our thoughts and emotions. Your speech begins to testify to the condition of your heart and then you will find yourself speaking in negative absolutes.

"No one loves me."
"Everyone has turned their back on me."
"I will never forgive him/her."
"I can't live without them."

Your thoughts can easily become polluted by your emotions. Your emotions will eventually determine your beliefs. And your beliefs will dictate your behavior. If you are not careful you will begin to agree with the lies that are being spoken into your spirit. Then, those lies become your reality. You cannot accept this as your plight and must use your own weapons to fight.

Our Spiritual Weapons

While the enemy has a plethora of weapons to use against the children of God, God has given us weapons of warfare to use as well. It is during times of distress that they are sharpened, revealed, and often manifested. Ephesians 6:10-20 provides us with a description of the armor of God and our personal arsenal of weapons to use against the enemy. Armor is used by the military to protect the body in battle. The armor is placed strategically to provide protection to the areas of vulnerability to the mortal body.

However, Paul encouraged us to put on God's whole armor that will enable us to be able to withstand the schemes of the devil. God's armor is designed to protect our hearts, our faith and our relationship with God. This is what the enemy targets through his "wiles" or schemes. If he cannot kill you physically, he will attempt to kill you spiritually. If he cannot kill you spiritually, he will get you to kill your own purpose through unrighteous living. The devil doesn't want your things he wants your life. The devil doesn't want the house that you live in, he wants to remove the spirit that you abide in. Jesus says in John 15:4, *"Abide in me, and I in you..."* (NKJV)

The ultimate goal in the devil's web of plots and plans is to remove Jesus, your Savior, from your life. The enemy will use tragedy, trauma, divorce, abuse and other issues of life to accomplish this deadly goal. Anything in your life that brings God glory, the enemy will target for destruction. A godly marriage, godly children, a tithe-giving budget, a holy body and spirit-filled faith walk just to name a few. However, God has not left us defenseless. There are many weapons of spiritual warfare that can be used, but I will only touch on three in this book that I used the most during that particular season: *true worship, praying in the Spirit,* and *praying God's Word.*

Worship as a Weapon

My first experience with spiritual weapons was when I was pregnant with my first son. I had experienced two emotionally painful miscarriages and suffered through six years of infertility prior to his birth. There was a moment in my first trimester when I no longer felt pregnant. I woke up in the middle of the night and I did not feel the normal pregnancy symptoms. The last time I felt that way I was having a miscarriage. Consequently, I went into a panic and retreated to the couch in the living room so that I didn't disturb my husband. I cried and even yelled at God. I couldn't believe it was happening to me again, and I felt as if I was going to lose my mind. Then, God told me that the only thing my womb had ever known is death and that I didn't know what it felt like to have life growing in me. Therefore, I could not use how I *felt* as a barometer for life.

At that moment, I realized that the battle was in my mind and I had to fight. I began to focus my thoughts on God and began to worship. As long as my thoughts were of God and only God, I couldn't think negatively. This gave me peace in my mind. As my pregnancy progressed, I had moments of fear but I would just begin to worship God, forgetting about myself and then peace would overtake me once again.

Authentic worship is neither about you nor me. True worship is about God and for God. When you make your worship all about God and don't even utter the word "I" you find yourself in another realm. The enemy cannot speak to you when your mind is worshipping God. Lies cannot penetrate your spirit when you are in the heavenly realms.

Our worship protects our mind and our spirits from intrusion. Worship is not a melody; it is a position, a posture and a prayer to God. Worship is exalting God, glorifying God's name and character. Worship reminds your spirit of God's attributes of holiness, lovingness and powerfulness. This kind of worship escorts you to the throne room of God and invites you into God's presence. When you change your atmosphere in worship, you are being changed in the spirit.

Even though we are human, we are spirits clothed in mortal bodies. When we are worshipping God in spirit and in truth, we are communing with God in the most intimate way. When we present ourselves to God in the truth of who we are, where we are and what we are feeling, God mobilizes the spiritual troops to defeat the enemy of our soul.

In 2 Chronicles 20, Jehoshaphat and the children of Israel had a huge army of enemies against them. The Lord spoke through Jahaziel and encouraged them not to be afraid of the massive army because the battle did not belong to them, but to God. (2 Chronicles 20:15)

In response to this, Jehoshaphat did two things: First, he bowed down with his face to the ground and worshipped the Lord. Then, he appointed men to sing to the Lord and to praise Him while they headed toward the army. While they sang praises to God, their enemies were defeated. Simply singing about the goodness of God can defeat the enemy and bring victory. There are many moments when I will plug in my headphones and listen to worship music and it changes my spirit and my mood from heaviness to contentment.

Worship as a weapon, influences your mind, encourages your faith and changes your emotions. It also positions you to hear from God regarding the strategy for your victory in the battle. If you use this weapon in your warfare watch how ineffective the enemy's weapons become in your life. You can also combine worship with intercession as an even stronger instrument of warfare.

Praying in the Spirit as a Weapon

"Likewise the Spirit also helps in our weaknesses. For we do not know what we should pray for as we ought, but the Spirit Himself makes intercession for us with groanings which cannot be uttered."

Romans 8:26 (KJV)

Praying in the Spirit is one of the most effective yet least utilized weapons of our warfare. The Spirit searches our hearts and intercedes for us according to God's will. When we pray in the Spirit, the Spirit will intercede for us and articulate to God words we cannot utter. This is probably the highest form of communication our spirit can have with God. There are times when we can't speak about everything we are feeling or have needs that we don't even know about. However, the Spirit will intercede on our behalf. This is vital during times of distress and can be very helpful during moments of internal turmoil.

Praying in the Spirit also builds us up in the faith. Paul admonishes us in Ephesians 6:18 to pray in the Spirit on all occasions. Praying in the Spirit doesn't always mean speaking in tongues. If you do not have or use a heavenly language that speaks in an unknown tongue, according to the word of God, your groaning will be made audible to Him.

I have a sister-in-love (no longer in-law) who I tease all the time about her wailing in the spirit. When she gets before the throne of God and she can't use her heavenly language she will begin to simply wail and she sounds like a wounded dog on steroids. However, the sound of her spirit calling out to God may seem odd to others, but I guarantee you that her spirit is touching the very heart of God and demons are taking flight from her situation.

Since I am not a doctor, I cannot prescribe any pharmaceuticals, but when speaking with Christians who are hurting, I do prescribe praying in the spirit. *(Jude 1:20, Ephesians 6:18 and Romans 8:26)* This is a strategy of warfare that can be used especially during high times of emotional distress. When your mind and emotions are raging out of control you are left alone and inconsolable by words. However, when the Spirit begins to pray it overrides the fleshy prayers and changes the trajectory of your emotions. Praying in the Spirit will strengthen you, encourage you and help you along in the journey. It will help you defeat the weapons of the enemy as your spirit is edified.

Regardless of how you may feel, you have the power of God in you to change the course of an enemy's attack. As you pray in the spirit, you may find that your position will switch from defensive to offensive. You might have entered in from a position of defense or weakness. However, when you are in the bowels of prayer God will exchange your weaknesses for His strength, giving you the power to not only fight, but win.

The Word as a Weapon

When we put on the armor of God, there are two things we place in our hands. One is the shield of faith and the other is the sword of the Spirit. A shield is a defensive weapon while the sword is an offensive weapon. The sword of the Spirit is the Word of God.

Throughout centuries, people have used the bible as a weapon of oppression instead of the liberation as it was created to be. The Word of God is extremely powerful and should be used to teach, encourage, and heal. It is a weapon against the devil and the devil alone. When you take God's Word and pray it in faith, God is obligated to answer God's Word. It is often said, that God does not answer your prayers, instead God answers God's Word. Therefore, when you pray, it is necessary for you to pray God's Word. This may sound elementary for us Christians, but when you find yourself in a place of darkness, our normal spiritual practices suffer.

Days after the news, I just laid in the bed with an old beat up King James Bible in my hands, and when I didn't know what to do with myself; I would just open it up and read. My Bible would always open to the Psalms. I finally found myself a companion to my pain and suffering in the scripture. I was able to connect to David and other writers of the Psalms as they vented their hearts to God. My heart now cried out to God as well and I no longer felt alone in my pain. During grief counseling sessions, people often ask me for scriptures that they can read in the bible. Instinctively, I know they are looking for someone or something that can relate to their pain because they feel as I did, that no one understands what they are going through.

I soon realized from reading the Psalms that each cry birthed a hope and that hope grew into victory, the same victory that I wanted in my life. That's how I took praying the Word of God to an entirely different level in my life and used God's word against the enemy. So when the enemy told me that no one loves me or everyone has left me, I learned to fight back with, *"God is with me. He will never leave me nor forsake me."* (See Deuteronomy 31:6, 8, Joshua 1:5 and Hebrews 13:5)

Worshipping God, praying in the Spirit and praying God's Word are just a few weapons that can be used in warring against the enemy that war against us. All of them require getting out of our natural mind and using our spiritual beings to completely focus on God. We are not always responsible for some of the thoughts that enter into our mind, but we are responsible for them staying there. Our words are powerful and we can win against the enemy by speaking the Word of God over our situations, to God in prayer and to the enemy during war. If life and death rests in the power of the tongue, we simply must make a choice to choose life with our lips. Even with the smallest muscle in our body we can defeat all weapons of mass torture.

❧ Journey Steps ❧

More weapons of mass torture: Dreams, good memories, bad memories, anniversaries, songs, scents (perfumes, colognes), photos, clothes, cars, bad theology, tradition, depression, suicidal thoughts, fear, reliving events, doubt, anger, guilt and shame.

❧ *Confession:* I will not allow any weapon designed to torture me to prevail in my thoughts. I take captive every negative thought, feeling and emotion and cast it away from my heart, mind and spirit.

❧ *Application:* Identify the specific weapons that are torturing your mind and spirit. Make your confession and pray daily against them prospering and establishing a root into your heart and spirit.

❧ *Prayer Starter:* Dear God, please expose every weapon that has been formed to assassinate my hopes, abort my purpose and kill my spirit. Lift up a hedge of protection around me that will cover my heart, mind, and spirit and allow my worship and prayers to usher me into your presence.

❧ *Scripture Meditation:* Psalm 91, Ephesians 6:10-20, Jude 1:20, 1 Peter 5:8, Romans 12:1-2, Proverbs 18:21

3

Grace in the Shadow of Death

"Yea, though I walk through the valley of the shadow of death, I will fear no evil; For You are with me; Your rod and Your staff, they comfort me."

Psalm 23:4 (KJV)

Every day, I seemed to walk around my house with a long, red, cotton robe that had been in my closet for years. Each day seemed like a foggy, fall morning on repeat. Words felt unimportant and doing anything felt futile. I was on automatic pilot and truly on the verge of crashing. My sister-in-love along with a few friends set up a schedule and lovingly watched and cared for me around the clock so I wouldn't be alone. One morning, I went to take a long shower just so I could cry and not be heard or seen for a few minutes. After setting the water temperature, I stepped into the shower and cried. I slid down to the floor of the shower and watched my tears camouflage themselves with the cascading water from the shower head. My tears trickled into the drain along with my failing strength. Suddenly, my spirit quietly began to stir. And, it stirred. It stirred and the Holy Spirit began making intercession for me.

As I stepped out of the shower, I continued praying in the Spirit and I went directly to my bedroom. I didn't allow anyone to stop me, speak to me or interrupt this direct line of communication that opened up in my spirit. I walked to my bedroom window where the sun was piercing through my room. God made an appointment with my spirit and announced Himself through the sunshine. In the window I felt the warmth of the sun's rays penetrate my wet skin and it dried the salty tears rolling down my cheeks. As I stood there in the window I noticed the shadow that was cast in my room behind me. With a quiet spirit, I waited. I arrived to my appointment and I was ready to listen.

What is Lurking in Your Shadow?

Do you remember when you were a kid and saw your shadow outside while playing? Shadows were a mystery and sometimes frightening because they seemed to follow you everywhere. Eventually, we would learn in school that a shadow is a dark area produced by a body or an object coming in between the light and the surface. Shadows shouldn't be scary but when tragedy, trauma and other painful circumstances strike our life, we find ourselves glaring into the dark shadow that surrounds us.

Living in the shadow of death is the darkest, loneliest place for anyone to live. Your world becomes that dark shadow which gets larger and larger. Your mind becomes a breeding ground for depression, stagnation and self-pity. A cycle of despair keeps your mind replaying events, conversations, emotions and hurts. In this shadow of death is where the weapons of mass torture are the most effective and it all takes place in the mind and heart.

When I learned about a suspected infidelity in my marriage, the first thing I did before I confronted my husband was pray. I prayed until there was a peace in my heart. Even though there were signs that any woman should have seen, I refused to allow my mind to go to what I called that "dark place" where emotions overtake all sensibility. In that dark place, my mind would have started wandering and replaying conversations and events, picturing who, when and where and torturing myself with information that I didn't have nor could verify.

Some people when they are angry would say that all they see is red before they go into a fit of rage. I didn't want to get to red and I definitely didn't want to see black. I even refused to allow my mind to pronounce him guilty and hoped there was an explanation that would explain away what I had been told. Unfortunately, our conversation didn't yield a confession or an acknowledgement. Most women would have went in swinging, cussing, throwing and yelling, but I prayed and went in with peace, a soft voice and a forgiving heart. I didn't know what my husband had done, but I knew his heart was to stay with me, and his son as a family so I was content with that and knew we would work through whatever happened.

Unfortunately, that opportunity of grace I was ready to give was never seized. Unbeknownst to me at the time, my husband was living in his shadow of guilt and shame. I didn't realize this because for the past six months prior to his death he was the most accommodating, friendly, loving husband and father we had ever experienced. For the first time in our marriage with our son, I felt like we were truly enjoying each other as a family. He was doing all the fatherly things with his son and the husbandly things with me, his wife. He no longer made excuses, worked late or a lot of overtime. He was present and enjoying our company. Nevertheless, he was being tortured with the guilt of his infidelity and had suffered in a quiet shame about what he had done. To make matters worse I became pregnant, and miscarried for the third time in our marriage and was completely devastated.

One night, he came home from work and found me sobbing on the bathroom floor holding a cup of a tiny dead fetus. That night he held me as I cried in bed, but I could tell he was uncomfortable. The next day he was so indifferent towards me that I began to feel bad for him. I thought to myself he must be in an incredible amount of pain as well. I later realized it was guilt that caused him to withdraw from me after the miscarriage. I am convinced the enemy tortured him with words like, *"You got her pregnant and your wife just miscarried."*

It was guilt and shame that no one knew about because he didn't talk about his feelings. It was difficult for him to talk about what was on his heart to anyone. He would talk about everything under the sun, except for his inner most thoughts. Clearly, what he had done was not representative of his character and even his relationship with God, but the enemy used that as ammunition to torture his soul. He lived in the shadow of guilt, shame and its deadly silence. What kind of dark shadow are you living in? Is it anger, resentment, sorrow, abandonment or something else? If your shadow could speak right now, what would it say?

Crisis is a breeding ground for generational curses to manifest.

The Silent Shadow

Shadows are not designed to be permanent and living there will eventually kill your wounded spirit. It is a lonely place to be and others do not often recognize it because you may mask your feelings with lies that everything is okay with you while denying the truth. Eventually you start believing the lies you have told yourself and stay in bondage to your sin, anger, hurt or your grief. Healing can only take place when we admit there is hurt, pain or sin that needs to be healed. Regardless of what caused your pain, it is still valid and needs to be worked through.

Statistics say that 54% of sexual assaults go unreported. The last thing a person wants to do after being sexually assaulted is talk about it, re-live it and be blamed for it. However, the worst thing she or he could do is not talk about it, or report it. When you don't discuss a pain or confess a fault, you will eventually internalize the pain, shame, anger and guilt. When you internalize the pain, it will manifest itself in different behaviors and attitudes. Eventually, if it is not dealt with, it will recycle into the next generation and become a generational curse. The cycle is vicious. Crisis is a breeding ground for generational curses to manifest.

As a result of what I experienced, I made a decision as a parent to be completely honest with our past and the details surrounding my late husband's death to our son. It would be a greater injustice for him and me if I were to hide or falsify the facts. People who keep secrets to protect someone are usually only protecting themselves. Keeping secrets or hiding our pain doesn't bring healing to anyone involved; instead it usually creates a new pain in someone else.

When the events of that fateful day happened, I initially made a decision not to reveal the attack on my life or the affair to his siblings and to anyone else that didn't know. I wanted his character and integrity to be intact not just for him, but for his legacy. Specifically, I didn't want his brothers to think any different of the older brother they looked up to all their life. But most of all, I didn't want people to forget how he lived because of how he died. Even our spiritual leaders, agreed with the decision I made and one even grilled me on who knew about those particular details. His intent was to keep those details contained to those few and bury the facts with those that knew. Sadly, this is very common in our families and in the Church.

The Church is a refuge and place of healing for those that are hurting. However, often in order to protect a family name or to save someone from embarrassment the Church will encourage someone to keep certain things to themselves. It seems harmless and done in good will, but it eventually becomes a seed that will germinate into a full grown tree with branches, leaves and fruits of secrets.

Why do you think we have adult women and men with a history of sexual promiscuity and making poor relationship decisions? Sometimes it stems from an early childhood abuse that they weren't allowed to talk about or was denied. That little person withdraws from the light of society and hides in the shadow and pain of their abuse and their healing process becomes delayed for decades until life forces them to confront the issue.

Sadly, my late husband's family could not handle the embarrassment and reality of what had happened and began making up stories to cover up the painful truth. For weeks, family and friends were told that my husband was just missing, creating false hope in those that wanted him alive. The church family was told that there was an "incident" involving one of our family members and even after his home going service months later, the truth of his death wasn't acknowledged. I did not blame nor fault the church because at that time I needed and wanted that privacy. I literally couldn't handle any more burdens.

Even now, it is extremely difficult to be this transparent with the most painful and embarrassing events in my life, but God promised me that when I did, it would set the captives free and bring healing to those who are bound and living in the shadow of death.

Silencing the hurt does not heal the heart.

Exposing the Dark

A month after the "incident" we received a tip regarding an unidentified body in the morgue and went to identify the badly decomposed corpse that I had to identify as my husband. The gruesome image and stench will forever be embedded into my memory. To this day, the thing that crippled my emotions the most was signing a piece of paper acknowledging that the unidentified body was that of my 41-year old husband and I was his wife. It seems like such a harmless procedure but it devastated me. That is not a document any wife or parent wants to sign or acknowledge.

I left the morgue and traveled an hour and half back home, over the bridge he jumped just a month prior. I walked back over the threshold of the house we bought together and God began to speak to me. I had never heard such aggression in the voice of God until He began to speak into my spirit regarding this situation.

The first thing God told me was that I was going to have to go into warfare against the spirits that warred against my husband: the spirits of guilt and shame.

Next, God showed me how I had to expose my husband's enemy and keeping secrets was not acceptable to God. God was angry with all the secrets and issues our family had been hiding and had swept under the carpet. It was then I remembered the prophetic word God gave me several months prior that something major and devastating was going to happen in our family and it was going to be an opportunity for confession. The message was clear, God wanted confession and all the secrets to stop. I had even called all my sisters-in-law who were spiritual warriors and told them so we could prepare ourselves. I just had no idea at the time, the event would initiate from my household.

Through your painful journey, you have to be fearless enough to fight and yet vulnerable enough to expose the dark and the fear it causes. If you are hiding pain, abuse, shame or something else, you will never be able to be healed from it until you expose it. Here is the thing I need you to remember – God knows. God knows what happens even if people don't. You don't have to hold a press conference, write a long Facebook post announcing your pain, but you do have to talk with God.

Do not allow your current circumstances to cause spiritual amnesia.

God's Grace

I've learned that God loves us too much to allow us to remain in the darkness of our pain. God cannot heal a wound that we do not offer to Him to heal. Healing doesn't begin when we hurt. Healing begins when we admit, or confess we have a hurt and then present ourselves and our afflictions to the Doctor. Psalm 34:19 says, *"Many are the afflictions of the righteous, but the Lord delivers him out of them all." (NKJV)*

Recovering from a tragedy, traumatic experience or death of a loved one can only be proceeded by healing. The healing process is a journey. It takes place over time and will lead to recovery, restoration and wholeness under the Doctor's supervision. I know that when we have been down for so long, up seems like a mission impossible. Friends and family don't understand the place where you now live, and you often can't articulate its depth, but there is help in the shadow. That help is called grace.

When God allowed me to look back to the day that my life was gutted like a fish, God pointed something out that I did not see in the beginning. Although I found myself literally in the shadow of death and anticipated my demise, I did not feel death approaching. Why? I wasn't alone. God was with me all the time. God was with me in my valley of the shadow of death just like the scripture states. We often overlook this reality because of the pain and despair that we feel during our time in the valley and the eclipse of our shadow. No matter how high or how low, God is there. Don't forget that. When God says, I will never leave you or forsake you. Don't forget that. When it doesn't feel like anyone else is there, God is there. Don't forget that. Do not allow your present circumstance to cause spiritual amnesia.

Finding New Perspective in the Shadow

When the sun goes down every night, it doesn't retreat into a dark abyss. It simply rises in another place, over another country. Therefore, the sun is always shining but you will only be able to see it based upon your geographic location.

Midnight is the darkest hour of the day, but the sun is still shining someplace else. When you are in your life's darkest hour and living in your shadow, God is still there shining. However, you will not feel the warmth of His rays until you change your location and step out of that dark shadow into the light.

Through the calm of that day and the brightness of the sun, God began to speak to my heart regarding the life that I knew and the life that was now gone. In His monologue with my heart, God answered my every question and even the ones I did not inquire about. He allowed me to see how His plan for me was unfolding and that everything that I was going through was for His glory. Everything I was enduring was for His name's sake. Every promise that He promised me was about to come to pass but it could only come through these circumstances. All the things God told me that I would do years ago, I never understood how I would be qualified or experienced to do any of it.

Now, the puzzle pieces of my life were beginning to fit. The book He said that I would write now made sense. The auditoriums He showed me now had a meaning. Every fuzzy area of my life now became clear. Every pain in my heart now had a purpose. Every scripture that I read now had a new meaning. Every song I heard had a new message in the melody. It was like a spiritual awakening. I was being awakened to the second half of my life and was about to embark on the painful journey to get there. I just had no idea it would be through the pain and circumstances called "my life." It was then that I realized my soul had truly been anchored in God because He gave me a peace that passed all my understanding.

God will not waste your pain. God will not waste the opportunity to show Himself strong in your life. There is a purpose and a plan that God has for your life that did not end when your tragedy, trauma or loss occurred. At some point in time, you will see the manifestation of the promises of God in your life if you just hold on to God's hand. The journey may be long and hard, but it is worth going through to get to God's promises. How do you see yourself in the future? Still bound by yesterday's pain? Hopefully not. I know that it is hard, but you have to find the strength within to expose the dark and allow God to shine.

"Have mercy on me, O God, have mercy on me, for in you my soul takes refuge. I will take refuge in the shadow of your wings until the disaster has passed."

Psalm 57:1 (NIV)

Shadows in themselves aren't necessarily evil, just ask David. When he was on the run from Saul, he took refuge in the shadow of God's wing. In that moment in the window, during my divine appointment with God, I walked out from the shadow of death and into God's light. I found refuge and safety in the bosom of His Son's rays. So will you. If you are going to sit in a shadow, let it be under the safety of God's wingspan. It is in that safety that you can expose the dark, its pain; along with the shame, guilt, or pain that you have hidden from everyone else. When you step out of the darkness of your past, your sins and/or your hurt, mercy greets you at the door and ushers you into the throne room of grace.

Grace is more than the unmerited favor we learned about in Sunday school. Grace is the enabling power to be who you are called to be and to do what you are called to do. Grace accompanies us on our journey through the struggles and tragedies of our lives.

If someone told you that life as a Christian would be easy, they lied to you. Life is not easy, but with God's grace it is livable during hardship. God spoke these words to Paul, *"...My grace is sufficient for you, for my power is made perfect in weakness..."* (2 Corinthians 12:9, NIV)

This was a time of duress for Paul. At that time, Paul had an unclear "thorn in his flesh" that he begged God to remove three times. Paul was bitten by snakes, shipwrecked and imprisoned. His life wasn't easy, but he was taught how to rely on God's grace. His reply was, *"...That is why, for Christ's sake, I delight in weaknesses, in insults, in hardships, in persecutions, in difficulties. For when I am weak, then I am strong."*

When you do as Paul did, or even myself and rely on God's grace, your journey to healing and to the land of the living begins. It may be a long journey, a tiring marathon through emotions and obstacles along the way, but God's grace is with you, every painful step of the way.

❧ Journey Steps ☙

- ❧ *Confession:* I will to come out of the dark and abide in the shadow of the Almighty God. I will not allow sorrow, pain, sin, shame or _____ to prevent me from experiencing God's Grace, mercy and my abundant life.

- ❧ *Application:* Confess to God what you have been holding on to. Make a promise to yourself that you will release it thereafter. If you feel the need to talk it out, confide in someone you trust, and is spiritually strong enough to handle your experience and feelings. This person can be a friend, family member, Pastor, Minister, Counselor or a Professional. You simply start by expressing to them that you need a *listening* ear.

- ❧ *Prayer Starter*: Dear God, in my hurt, pain, and _____ I have hid myself from your presence. Please shine your light on me right now and expose every area of darkness, sadness, sickness, regret, pain or hurt that I have endured. Guide me from the darkness and into your marvelous light.

- ❧ *Scripture Meditation:* Psalm 23, 1 Peter 2, James 5:16, 1 John 1, Philippians 4:7

SECTION TWO

Your Journey

4

Navigating Destiny Detours

"For you, Lord, have delivered me from death, my eyes from tears, my feet from stumbling, that I may walk before the Lord in the land of the living."

Psalm 116:8-9 (NIV)

Who could forget the ominous grey skies and long back wind tunnel, racing towards that rural town, quickly approaching the quaint farm filled with horses, chickens and other farm animals. Debris is flying everywhere, animals are panicking and people are running to their storm shelters seeking refuge from the inevitable. With nowhere to hide and her family out of sight the young girl was forced to retreat into her house being rattled by the storm. Her house should have been a safe place. Her house should have provided relief from the storm but it was abruptly swept up into the air. The house that she called home was now in a dark, angry wind tunnel spinning unapologetically through the eye of the tornado.

While knocked out by debris, her fears silenced by unconsciousness until she finally awakes. The storm has ended. The house has landed. The skies cleared and the sun came out to shine as if it didn't see the havoc that nature's elements caused. She opens the front door and realizes she is no longer in Kansas. Although, she survived the storm, she is now a stranger in a foreign place. She takes her first steps confused, amazed and fearful. With her heart fixed on the home and world she left, she would now have to navigate through this new terrain.

While Dorothy is a fictional character from the movie *The Wizard of Oz*, we can relate to her incredible journey. Now that a tornado has hit your life, you find yourself in a world you didn't recognize but yet you are expected to navigate through this place to find your way back home. For Dorothy, finding her way home would prove difficult, but not impossible and she would have to overcome the detours along the way. In the end, she discovered that home was closer then she believed. However, before she could return home, she had a purpose to fulfill while she was in Oz. As her journey unfolds, the detours begin and her life seems to unravel. Can you relate?

Whether or not you feel like you are moving, you are definitely on the journey of your life. We are all on a journey, walking through this life that God has given us. Along this journey, we will be confronted with various ups and downs, mountain highs and valley lows. As believers in Christ, we journey through this life with heaven as our end. Along the way, we not only live for Christ but we become a witness so that others may know the love of Christ as well. As a member of the body of Christ, each of us has an assignment from God wherein we concentrate on a particular area, group of people etc. When we are all doing our part of Kingdom work, the whole earth will get to know Jesus and the God we serve. This is your purpose. This is your life's journey. However, there are some of life's tornados, hurricanes, hail-storms and other devastations that will cause a roadblock or detour you on our journey. These tragedies, traumas and great losses can disrupt your life to the point that it can detour your destiny.

When the unthinkable happens and you find yourself as a stranger in a new place one of two things can happen: you stay or leave. The place that you are in now is not a final destination. The hurt, the discomfort and pain of your situation is not the place that God has destined for you. You can either stay or you can leave. Some of you are thinking right now, *"Who would want to stay?"* While others are questioning, *"How do I leave?"* No one wants to stay in a negative place, but sometimes lack the strength, courage or strategy to leave. Then if they leave they are discouraged by the roadblocks and setbacks they encounter.

Navigating through destiny detours is not easy nor for the faint of heart. You are required to travel against the current and the wind, overcoming the elements that will slow you down or impede your journey. You have to defeat the giants in your path despite your limitations. You have to fight for the faith despite the doubts that run through your mind. You have to set your eyes on your help and not on the hill. You have to encourage yourself when no one else is around.

Just like Dorothy, one day Moses found himself a stranger in a new land with a destiny that was greater than his personal storm. Returning home would prove to be a lot more difficult for Moses and the obstacles and roadblocks more life threatening. The obstacles in Moses' life would not only danger his physical life but his destiny as well.

Three Assassinating Angels

When the enemy recognizes God's plan to use a person for the Kingdom of God, he attempts to kill them physically. The devil assigns assassinating angels to annihilate the purpose of God in our lives. As a part of a decree from Pharaoh, Moses was a part of an elaborate plot to kill Hebrew male children. God used the wisdom of his mother and the protection of the midwives to spare Moses' life. The enemy tried to kill Moses in order to prevent him from fulfilling his purpose in life, which was delivering the children of Israel.

When the enemy can't kill the physical person, he will subtly try to kill the spirit person. The devil sent three assassinating angels to abort the purpose, mission and destiny of Moses: rejection, fear and insecurities. Those same spirits are often used against us. In the medical field, abortion is the means of terminating a pregnancy before its full maturation and subsequent birth. If the enemy can cause you to abort your purpose, the death of your spirit will closely follow. Our human organs sustain our mortal bodies, but it is our spirit that is granted eternal life.

Insecurity

Trauma, tragedies and great losses in your life can cause you to feel insecure about who you are and the direction that God wants for your life. Our identities are wrapped up in our family life, church life and careers. When those identities are rocked by terrible circumstances we begin to question ourselves. Before the circumstances happened, you were confident of who you were in God and probably in the plan He had for your life. However, when life hit you hard, question marks appeared on everything. You have start questioning what to do with the broken pieces of your life. You don't feel like the strong, independent, faithful child of God. You feel weak, unconfident and unsure about life.

Insecurity is a subtle spiritual assassin that the enemy sends to kill your purpose and undermine your confidence. Insecurity doesn't sound very dangerous and yet it can be quite effective in preventing someone from actualizing and activating their assigned purpose. Our purpose is attached to other people. So if you are not walking in your purpose it affects the lives of other people. Insecurities imbed internal conclusions about ourselves that negates the reality of what is in us. Insecurities are lies about our abilities or identities that we have internalized. When you have lost confidence in yourself, you do not trust yourself with what God gives you to have or to do.

God met Moses in the backside of the desert and told him that he would deliver the Israelites from the hand of the Egyptians. Moses made excuses for why he wasn't a good candidate for the job. Ironically, Moses didn't mention his top-notch Egyptian education and the fact that he was raised as a Prince in the King's palace. Moses gave excuses not because he just did not want to do it, but he held onto insecurities that were the result of being rejected by his people before he left Egypt. Feelings of insecurity can prevent you from leaving the place that you are in and reaching your destination. It can keep you bound to an unfulfilled life, one that was not designed for you. Moses had a destiny to be the great deliverer of the Hebrews not only a shepherd from Midian. Insecurities are so dangerous that they could cause you to reject your own purpose. They can cause you to decide on another path and not fulfill the plan of God because they alter your vision of who you are.

You are more than what happened to you. You are more than the victim. You are more than who left you or died. You are not your circumstance. You are not your tragedy. You are not what you lost. You are the child of the eternal God. You are God's most precious gift in the earth. You are who God says you are. You are more than a conqueror. You are an overcomer and you are destined for greatness.

Rejection

While insecurities can cause one to attack one's self, rejection is an outward attack that is just as dangerous. Everybody will not understand your journey. People may not understand the strategy that God has given you to return back to the land of the living. The course may seem different, odd and unusual to them. It may require you to make changes that people find uncomfortable. People who don't see the plan that God has for your life will question your path and even reject it or you.

Rejection is another deadly, assassinating angel that targets your divine purpose and can detour you on your journey. All of us at one point in our lives have been the object of rejection. Rejection is like a vile, bitter poison to the soul. It maliciously eats away at a person's self-esteem, self-worth and self-identity. Rejection is like a poison to the heart. Once the fangs are removed, its venom remains and causes a debilitating paralysis to the central nervous system and ultimately death. There are two main reactions from people who suffer with the spirit of rejection.

Some people who are rejected, reject others as a defense mechanism. Rejected people erect walls and become snipers shooting toward anything or anyone that comes in their direction. The other reaction of rejected people is that they form co-dependent or unhealthy attachments to relationships in their quest to be accepted.

The worst form of rejection is when it stems from the person(s) you expected to love you. When family or spouses reject you it hurts more than any other source of rejection. When you feel unloved, the spirit of rejection finds an entry point into your soul and will ignite a poison of self-destruction.

There was a spirit of rejection that was assigned to me and fought me long and hard and even sent me a double-edge sword. I had my mom, our family and a few good friends for support. However, when I was rejected by other family, friends and ultimately my spouse, it left me feeling hopeless and useless as a human being. When an old associate came into my life and seemingly accepted me when no one else did I held on for dear life. Unfortunately, he also suffered from the spirit of rejection and used rejection as a means of defense and personal warfare. It was the worst combination and nearly killed me physically and spiritually. The danger in rejection is that it can be transferred from parents to children generationally and even through pregnancy.

Rejection has to be fought aggressively through prayer, and combated with affirmations and acceptance of who you are in God. In confronting my personal rejection and being ostracized by my husband's suicide I came to the decision to stop numerating all the people who left me and my son and counted instead, the few that remained. In doing so, I was able to embrace and be embraced by the true love of God. God's love doesn't leave nor forsake you. I began to understand how Jesus, the most rejected, felt when his brothers and disciples rejected him openly. Jesus exemplified the way to prevent bitterness from rejection from taking root. When His followers turned their backs on Him as participants and observers of His execution, Jesus responded, *"...Father, forgive them, for they do not know what they are doing." Luke 23:34, NIV.*

Perhaps you have been rejected by a spouse, which resulted in a divorce. Perhaps you have been rejected from social circles because of everything that you have lost. Perhaps you have been rejected by our judicial system whose laws do not protect you. Perhaps you been rejected by family because you have refused to be silent on a childhood abuse. Whatever the cause of the rejection, there is hope. The most important element of overcoming rejection is forgiveness.

I have found that forgiveness is the hardest to do when others haven't accepted responsibility or offered apologies. I learned that forgiveness has less to do about the other person(s) and everything to do about you. When you realize the power of forgiveness and its benefits you work toward it. Job's family and wealth was restored only *after* he prayed for his friends, also known as the "miserable comforters." The spirit of rejection doesn't leave easily and will come back often with assaults. However, prayer, fasting and reading God's word is the best defense in confronting rejection.

Fear

One of the most detrimental and commonly assigned assassinating angels or spirits is fear. Fear is used as a tactic to cause spiritual paralysis. By definition, paralysis is the loss of function and feeling or the power of voluntary motion. To paralyze something means to make it *powerless* or *inactive*. Fear is an overwhelming emotion caused by an intense expectation or awareness of danger. The spirit of fear immobilizes or paralyzes God's children and prohibits them from fulfilling their destiny, purpose and receiving the promises of God.

Moses was on the verge of allowing his destiny to die in the desert because of his insecurity, rejection and fear. However, he wasn't the only one. When the children of Israel were in the wilderness of Paran at Kadesh listening to the report of the spies, fear penetrated their hearts and kept them from wanting to enter into the Promised Land. Because of their faithlessness, complaints and rebellion God would not let them enter. That faithless generation had to die in the wilderness and they were not able to enjoy the sweetness of the fruit and ownership of their own land.

Forty years later, Joshua, the new leader sent two spies into the land to scout it out and came across Rahab who hid them from the King's men. I'm sure the men were surprised to have encountered someone that would protect them knowing they were spies. However, I would contend that they were more surprised that the people were actually afraid of them.

"...and she said to them, "I know that the Lord has given this land to you and that a great fear of you has fallen on us, so that all who live in this country are melting in fear because of you. We have heard how the Lord dried up the water of the Red sea for you when you came out of Egypt....When we heard it, our hearts melted and everyone's courage failed because of you, for the Lord your God is God in heaven above and on the earth below."
Numbers 2:9-11 (NIV)

The enemy is afraid of you fulfilling the plan of God for your life so he sends attacks to your mind. The enemy would rather you die in the dessert of unfulfilled promises and your bones decay in the valley of unallocated blessings. The abundant life that God wants us to have does not begin until we are living, breathing and walking in the purpose of God. You are not truly alive until you are living out your purpose. Jesus said in John 10:10,

"The thief comes not, but for to steal, and to kill, and to destroy. I am come that they might have life, and that they might have it more abundantly."

That abundant life is not about big homes, yachts and wealth but instead a purpose driven life active in the Kingdom of God.

Do not allow fear to keep you from moving out of the negative place that you are in. Do not allow anything that was not sent by God to keep you from your destiny, your purpose and God's plan for your life. The more you fight, the more you walk, the stronger you will become. Eventually, you will get to that new life after surviving what happened to you, but don't get discouraged when you arrive and it feels uncomfortable at first. Sometimes new is uncomfortable simply because it's new, just like a pair of shoes. Regardless, you still must leave anything from your past that wasn't designed to live in your present.

Re-Entering the Land of the Living

When you re-enter the land of the living or your predestined promise land you have to leave behind everything that died in the desert. Faithlessness cannot enter. Doubt cannot enter. Death cannot enter. Fear cannot enter. Rejection cannot enter. Insecurity cannot enter. You have to let go of who left, what hurt you, who died, etc. You have to let go of the pain, offense and un-forgiveness. I could never forget my late husband, but I had to learn how to let go of the pain his death caused me in order to begin living my new life and walk into my destiny.

While the old doubting, disobedient generation could not enter the Promised Land, two did. Caleb and Joshua. God told Joshua, *"Be strong and be courageous, because you will lead these people to inherit the land I swore to their forefathers to give them." Joshua 1:6*

You will have to fight some battles in order to maintain in your new territory or life. There will be giants in the land, but when God is your Commander-In-Chief, He instructs you, and makes sure you are prepared and victorious.

It is imperative to put our dark, stormy times into the proper perspective of our entire life. Navigating through turbulent times will be difficult, but if we acknowledge the obstacles and become aware of the detours, we will find our way back home, back to the land of the living and toward our destiny.

It easy to stay in pain after a while because you've become used to it. You become used to crying yourself to sleep at night. You can become accustomed to your grieving where it feels a part of life's routine. You can become habitual about replaying events over and over again. You can even be comfortable in your discomfort. Don't let pain be a crutch or an excuse for not moving away from the pain of the past. In order to move forward you have to confront the pain and the obstacles that keep you from moving forward. If you do not confront those areas in your life that cause you pain, you will find yourself dying to your yesterday instead of living for your tomorrow.

What keeps you in your past? What keeps you bound to your pain? What keeps you distracted from making plans for the future? Have you gone off the beaten path or off the grid? This is a great time to search your heart and identify what or who is in the way. The tragedy, trauma or loss was not designed to kill you. However, God can use it to steer you in the direction of your destiny.

I urge you to walk into the land of the living, with boldness being led by the power and authority of God each victorious step of the way. When the journey feels unbearable, remember God has given you grace for the journey. When you understand the grace that is upon your life, you will know that regardless of the terrain in your journey, God has graced you to go through it and reach your destiny.

⋄ Journey Steps ⋄

☙ Confession: I see the roadblocks and detours of _____ in my life and I shall not let them hinder me from reaching my healing, restoration and divine destiny.

☙ Application: Make a list of everything that is hindering you from moving forward. Pray for strength and deliverance in those areas daily until it is no longer an issue.

☙ Prayer Starter: Dear God, I have been going through a terrible storm in my life that has me feeling like everything is spinning out of control. I ask that you allow me to see all the things that hinder me from moving from this place. Please deliver me from my insecurities, the rejection, fears and anything that will detour me from my destiny. I trust you with my journey and to be a lamp to my feet so that I make this journey with your grace.

☙ Scripture Meditation: Romans 8:37-39, Jeremiah 29:11

5

The Road to Your Comeback

"I would have lost heart, unless I had believed that I would see the goodness of the Lord in the land of the living."

Psalm 27:13-14 (NKJV)

Everybody loves a great comeback. In any genre of movie we want to see the victim become the victor, the disgraced recover and the hero triumph over the villain. In sports, we want to see our favorite team or athlete emerge from a losing position to a winning one. Spectators love a great comeback, although they don't participate in the journey, they do rejoice in the victory without feeling all the misery. I love Naomi's comeback story.

At the intersection of Grief Street and Bitterness Lane, Naomi's story unfolds on a road in Moab. If you recall from chapter one, when she left Bethlehem, she was married with two sons. Over ten years later, she is now a stranger in Moab, childless and a widow with no protection, covering nor provision. However, Naomi heard that the Lord was providing food for his people in her hometown, Bethlehem of Judah. Naomi heard.

Listening for Directions

While in Moab, Naomi was being set up for her great comeback even though she didn't realize it at the time. First it started with her ability to still hear. In order for Naomi to hear about what the Lord was doing in her hometown, she had to hear from someone close to her. Sometimes when life drags us through the mud, we can become bitter and angry and we don't want to hear anything from anybody including God. We become inconsolable and discouraged. The well-meaning efforts of friends and family fall short of being helpful and feel more like a bother. We may isolate ourselves from the real world in order to avoid the reminder that our world has changed.

When our world is filled with turmoil and distress it becomes easy to stop praying, stop reading God's word and stop going to church. However, these are all the ways that we hear from God. When your prayer life is affected by your circumstances it becomes more difficult for God to affect change in those circumstances. If your heart is hardened from the pain and you cannot hear God's voice, then you cannot receive your encouragement or directions to get you out of that place called *There*.

When God gave me the charge to leave my home and move 1200 miles away, He instructed me every step of the way even down to the timing. In the midst of what I was going through I obeyed and walked in faith. Just like the children of Israel who were ready to go into the Promised Land after 40 years. God gave them specific instructions for that new season. If they were going to take over the territory and inhabit the land, they were going to have to obey His directives carefully. From the roads they had to travel to the method of warfare, God gave them specific instructions. You will need to do the same for this journey on the road to your comeback. When your heart has been through so much hurt and destruction, the last thing you need is to walk into an ambush or remain in the wilderness although your time has expired.

Whether you realize it or not, your comeback strategy has already been written and God's waiting for you to incline your ear to Him for directions. I strategically wrote and organized this book to not only offer encouragement but also practical tips to help you along the journey. Each chapter has scriptures and memory verses designed to keep you hearing from God for your particular situation. I encourage you to spend time daily allowing God to minister to your heart through scripture, songs or through worship. You may not feel like it, but once you begin you will find that your spirit is bigger than your feelings.

When you feed your spirit, your emotions will change. When you do this consistently, you become stronger. As you incline, or turn, your ear to God, you will be downloaded with directions for which road to take for your comeback. In the midst of being upset, don't stop praying, don't stop reading God's word and don't stop hearing from God. Naomi heard, then she prepared.

It is better to deal with the hurts of today, before they become luggage for tomorrow.

Preparations for the Journey

When Naomi heard about the provisions that were being made in Judah, she then prepared to return to her homeland. Before embarking on any trip, it is necessary to pack your bags. When I came to the same cross roads as Naomi and decided to leave New York for new horizons I had to pack up my entire house. This was a daunting task not only because of the laborious magnitude of packing in itself, but the emotional toll it took on me.

During the process of packing, purging takes place. You have to decide what to throw away versus what to keep. Packing and unpacking requires some discernment and some perseverance. Rummaging through old things and being forced down memory lane can be painful and joyous. Some items you can pack to bring with you and other things must be discarded.

Sometimes making those decisions creates new pains in the heart. I decided that I would discard the things that would bring me pain and keep the ones that brought me joy. It would have been easy to just throw everything away and start fresh, but I wanted to heal healthily and that meant going through the painful process. It meant leaving all the negativity behind me, and pressing forward. It meant leaving behind the pain of the things that hurt me. It meant not reliving my worst memories over and over again. It meant releasing the plans that *I* had for my future in exchange for God's plan. It meant leaving behind the anger, bitterness and fear. It meant leaving behind unforgiveness, pride and regret. None of those things were going to bring any value in my life, so I made a choice to leave them behind.

On the road to your comeback, there are some things that are necessary for you to leave behind. There are some things that you will even need to unpack before you take a step on that journey. We can become so comfortable in our discomfort that we hold onto our pain and pack it away. We pack away the hurt, pain, disappointments, broken promises and failures. For weeks, months and sometimes years we carry the burden of yesterday's pain. We know we can't stay in that hurting place, but we are too burdened down to move.

Often times we tend to brush issues and hurts under the carpet to avoid the pain, repercussions and the truth. Now, the pains of our past that we have packed away prevent us from reaching our destiny, our healing and our wholeness. It prevents us from reaching the place that God wants for us because we won't unpack and deal with the hurts of our yesterday.

It is better to deal with the hurts of today so that they do not become luggage for tomorrow. This requires taking an honest look into ourselves and making a decision to allow the healing process to begin. It also means identifying each hurt and attending to that hurt through specific prayers, scriptures and even counseling. Then do it again with the next issue, tackling each, one at a time.

When my world came crashing down in one day, I had to deal with unconventional grief, PTSD from the assault, the infidelity bombshell, being ostracized from family and friends, and my financial hardship. I had to tackle a long list from abandonment and rejection to grief and self-esteem. It was overwhelming thinking about it all at once, so I handled one issue at a time and found strength in each small victory. Running away from your problems are futile, but dealing with them is a lifesaver. Listening to the voice of God and unpacking the hurt are the first steps toward the road to your comeback. Naomi heard. Naomi prepared, then she left.

Everybody that attaches themselves to you has not been assigned to you.

Your Road

After Naomi heard what God was doing in Judah, Bethlehem, she made preparations and then left on the road to return home. She left Moab with her two daughters-in-law, Ruth and Orpah. It is unknown how far they went before Naomi thought it was the wrong decision to bring them. Naomi told them to turn back. At first they both refused but Orpah turned back and Ruth pleaded her case to go to Judah with Naomi.

I won't begin a negative discourse on how quickly or why Orpah turned back. However, it is important to understand that on your road to your comeback, not everybody will be able to go where God is directing you to go. Everybody that attaches themselves to you has not been assigned to you. You have to discern who is sent to distract you instead of assist you toward reaching your destiny and divine purpose.

The same people that were with you before your trauma, tragedy and loss, may not be the same ones you encounter on your journey back to the land of the living, and that's okay. There are people that are just not capable of walking with you during certain seasons of your life. God may send strangers or even the unsuspecting associate to be the one that speaks life into you and walks with you.

One day, God had a woman who was my former Christian Education teacher to call me. She heard the news about what happened to our family in spite of her relocation. In talking to me, she was the first and only person to address a hurt that was still buried at the time. She knew that if I didn't address that hurt that my self-esteem, self-confidence and future relationships were at stake. I silently wept on the phone and couldn't even bring myself to tell her what damage already occurred.

I had already begun spiraling looking for acceptance and wholeness in someone who was just as broken as I was. Although, I hadn't spoken to her in years that one conversation opened my eyes to more heart work that I needed to do. It wasn't the people that were the closest that were able to help me. It was the people that God sent to me.

Leaving the place that you are in sometimes means leaving the people and things that no longer bring value into your life. Walking towards healing and walking towards a renewed life means leaving behind dead relationships and dead issues. When Naomi left from Moab to travel to Judah, she had to pass the Jordan River and the Dead Sea.

The Dead Sea is formed by the waters from the Jordan River and other small streams. It is also known as the Salt Sea. There is no outlet or outflow from the Dead Sea. It is known as the lowest and saltiest place on earth laying 1,300 feet below sea level. Waters come in, but the only way out is through evaporation (seven million tons daily) and only fresh water can escape through this route. Therefore, the salinity and mineral content of the water just increases. Because of this, nothing can live in these waters, hence its name. However, it is virtually impossible to sink in it as well. Therefore, you cannot live in the Dead Sea. Nothing can. However, nothing can sink in it either. The Dead Sea is designed to keep things from sinking.

Now, imagine the very place that you thought you would die can also be the place designed to keep you from drowning. In this place that you are in, you may feel like you are dead inside, but there is a stream of living water that exists on the inside of you that will keep you from sinking and drowning.

"Whoever believes in me, as the Scripture has said, streams of living water will flow from within him."

John 7:38, NIV

If you are not sinking, nor swimming, then you must be floating. If you are floating, then you are on your back which requires you to look up. Are you looking up to the hills from which comes your help? This is what will keep you from sinking. This is what will keep you focused on the journey ahead.

You might not be swimming, running, walking or crawling right now, but you are still alive. You are still able to hear God's voice for directions. You still have the ability to make the necessary preparations for your journey. You still have the opportunity to leave that place of hurt and get on the road to your personal comeback. Nevertheless, getting on that road will require some courage.

Courage to Comeback

When Naomi returned to Judah, she returned bitter. Naomi even told people to call her Mara, which means "bitter." Naomi, left Judah full, with a husband and children, but returned home empty. Her hopes, her future and livelihood died in Moab and bitterness set in on the road back to Judah.

Naomi might have been bitter but she was also courageous. In spite of being talked about and returning empty, she didn't allow pride to keep her from returning home. Nelson Mandela defined it best when he said,

"I learned that courage was not the absence of fear but the triumph over it. The brave man is not he who does not feel afraid, but he who conquers fear."

Nelson Mandela

Simply stated, courage is doing things afraid. You may have to start over. You may have to move. You may have to change your profession. You may have to relearn how to walk. You may have to raise your children alone. You may have to live a new life that you didn't see yourself living a few years ago. Be courageous, conquer your fears and move forward. Don't give up, keep pressing, keep walking and keep believing. Your comeback is not for you alone. Your comeback is going to bless you and others along the way. Getting on the road to your comeback is about pursuing your destiny and purpose in God's Kingdom.

Naomi returned to Judah and began working on a plan that would allow her daughter-in-law to remarry. Ruth would eventually marry Boaz, Naomi's kinfolk, and they had a son, which was attributed to Naomi. By the end of the book of Ruth, Naomi's life completely turned around. Her story is a reversal of fortune story. She lost, but she gained it back.

You might have suffered loss, but you will experience gain again. You might have suffered hurt, but your joy is coming back. You might be broken, but your wholeness is coming back. The life you knew may be gone, but a new, better life is coming back. Listen for God's instructions. Make all necessary preparations, leave that place of There and get on our road to your comeback. Your story may still be in development, but I believe you have a great comeback story in the making.

✥ Journey Steps ❧

- *Confession:* I declare that my latter days will be greater than my former days. I will put my past behind me and press toward the mark of the high calling in Christ Jesus.

- *Application:* Make a list of items in your life that needs to be unpacked and dealt with spiritually and practically. Identify which items you can work on and/or which areas you may need help or counseling. Then do the work.

- *Prayer Starter:* Dear God, I am grateful for the life that you have given me. In spite of everything that I have endured, I pray that you give me the courage to stay in the race and run it with perseverance. Help me to hear your voice so that I may walk according to your will. I shall make a comeback.

- *Scripture Meditation:* Psalm 121:1, John 7:38, Isaiah 55:3, Acts 27:22, Job 42:12, Haggai 2:9

6
Living on Hope until Help Arrives

"We wait in hope for the Lord; he is our help and our shield."

Psalm 33:20 (NIV)

Snow flakes began falling on the ground on the cold winter morning of his home going service. The funeral home put up a tent and positioned chairs by the gravesite for myself, and his parents as all our other family and friends huddled around us. For a few moments, time stood still. I sat in that chair staring at the suspended casket and the empty grave that awaited its company. The moment had finally arrived. The moment I dreaded the most was here. The moment that marked the occasion that death did us part arrived.

I knew the body that was in the casket was a badly decomposed corpse that was battered against the rocks alongside a grim river. I knew the spirit and soul of the man that I married was not present in that casket. But as I sat there, the widow, no longer the wife, I pondered my husband's final decision. After letting out a loud cry, I wept softly and whispered, *"I'm sorry."* I knew he couldn't hear me, but my heart overwhelmed my senses.

For a moment, I felt survivor's remorse. We were both Christians. Yet, I was the one sitting in the chair and he was lying in a casket. My heart ached and I was so sorry he lost the one thing he needed the most. He resigned the one thing that would keep him alive during hard times – hope. I couldn't help but analyze my hope tank. Where was my hope? As a born again believer and a woman of faith, I didn't know how it felt to live without hope until the day he died.

On that fateful day, my hope was that we would somehow be reunited in a hospital late that night. I daydreamed about the tears that we both would shed and the promises made to each other to work through the events that led us to that day. Unfortunately, my daydream turned into a nightmare instead. My hope of seeing him alive dissipated with the dawn of each new day. My hope of having more children and getting married again disappeared. My hope of the happily-ever-after died a very tragic death. Any hope that I had of returning to a normal, happy life faded with every tick on the clock.

I couldn't help but wonder how long my husband lived without hope. I wondered when he resigned his hope. I tried to return to the recesses of my mind for warning signs of this resignation. However, I realized given the timing of events, this wasn't premeditated by any means, although there had been some internal struggles long before that day. I believe it was on that day that the guilt and shame, which had imprisoned his hope, forced him to retreat from this life. When he looked at the consequences of his sins, I believe he foresaw a future he could not bear.

When a person loses faith for the future, he/she loses the faith to face it and does not have the strength to build it. They are left with a sick heart dying of hopelessness. In his book, *The Power of Hope*, author and teacher, Dutch Sheets describes how the sick heart deteriorates through various stages.

- *Discouragement* – the early stage of this disease.
- *Confusion* – we begin to question ourselves, our dreams, and God's promises.

- *Unbelief* – hope is now lost and expectation is gone.

- *Disillusionment* – which usually involves questioning even the character of God.

- *Bitterness* – wherein with deep feelings of resentment we blame God, others, and maybe even ourselves.

- *Cynicism* – a complete loss of faith and hope.[2]

Tragedy, trauma and great loss can cause even the strongest of faith to become weary with a sick heart. Hope deferred happens to us all at some point in our lives. We all deal with unfulfilled or shattered dreams during the course of life. Just like the common cold, we all get sick, from time to time. However, we all have different methods of treating our sickness, which determines how quickly we recover or if we recover at all. If you want to know if your heart is sick from hope deferred, you can diagnose your own symptoms.

The Diagnosis

A person with a sick heart finds themselves on "automatic," just going through the motions, emotionless, and doing and saying whatever is needed to make it through the day. They feel empty and lifeless. They are unable to be encouraged or comforted with words. All words of comfort and encouragement are met with doubt and negativity. The sick and diseased heart has a variety of ranges. It ranges from discouragement to depression. Doubt to Cynicism. Grief to suicidal tendencies.

When I look at all of these symptoms, I not only recognize my late husband's demise, but I am able to trace my own as well. I am able to acknowledge where my own heart became sick of discouragement, confusion and bitterness. I found myself drowning in a sea of despair. I became weary, breathless and tired. Tidal waves of hopelessness crashed into my faith and rattled my prayers on a daily basis. However, something anchored my soul that prevented me from going under and losing all hope.

> *"Hope is to the heart what seeds are to the earth. Without hope life is sterile, unfruitful. Without out it dreams won't be conceived; destinies won't be realized."*
> Dutch Sheets, The Power of Hope

The Sick Heart

Losing hope doesn't occur overnight. You don't go to bed full of hope and wake up hopeless the next morning. When you have hope, you are operating on a full tank of everything that is associated with hope. You are full of love, faith, confidence and peace, just to name a few. However, when you resign your hope and it is gone, something must take its place. Hopelessness leaves a void that requires something to replace it.

When you begin to lose hope, doubt is rooted and fear springs up like an unwanted weed in a garden of expectation. A hopeless heart is governed by its own negative reasoning instead of relying on the faithfulness of God. It is in our hopelessness that we decide that we will never marry or find love again. It is in our hopelessness that we find a broken relationship as a security blanket. It is in our hopelessness that we decide that we will never be happy again. It is in our hopelessness that we lose confidence in the omnipotent God.

I will never forget during a sermonic message, my Pastor, Dr. Eugene L. Gibson said, "when you worry, you declare three things: God doesn't care. God doesn't know. God can't fix it." This statement blew my mind and continues to ring in my ear anytime I begin to worry or feel anxious about a situation. While this is such a powerful truth to expose, one must recognize that the declaration is unlawful and uncharacteristic of God. The bible declares that God is Omnipresent, Omniscient and Omnipotent. God is everywhere. God knows all. God is all powerful.

"Cast all your anxiety on him because he cares for you."

1 Peter 5:7 (NIV)

The truth of the matter is God cares, God knows and God can fix it. If you are reading this book, I believe that you still have a thread of hope. I believe that you know God cares about you. It may not always be evident in your thoughts, your emotions and your prayers, but somewhere, hope is anchoring your soul.

Defining Hope

For many years, I have questioned the definition of hope. I often pondered how hope differed from faith. I recall as a teenager asking my mom. As an adult, I have even asked my Seminary Professors, and Pastors, looking for an answer that resonated with me. Interestingly enough, I found the best answers through my personal experiences coupled with what I've been learning about hope.

Hope is the beginning, the genesis, the starting point of an optimistic future. It is the embryo of all dreams and expectations. It is the expectation of something good with an indication of certainty. Hope serves as an incubator where faith is formed. Hope in its seed form carries confidence in something. Hope is only hope because it is rooted in something greater than itself. Faith needs hope to survive in between the seed and the fruit. When hope stays in the incubator long enough, confidence develops, courage manifests and faith emerges.

Everyone has a measure of hope. The world puts its hope or expectation into worldly things, but as believers in Christ we put our hope in the promises of God. That is the root of our hope in which we have our confidence and full assurance of our faith.

"Faith is the confidence that what we hope for will actually happen; it gives us assurance about things we cannot see."

Hebrews 11:1 (NLT)

Hope matures into faith and faith is the manifestation of hope. You can hope and not have faith, but you certainly cannot have faith without hope. Hope breathes for you when tragedy, trauma and loss leave you on life support. Hope sustains you until help arrives.

When Naomi left for Judah because she heard the Lord was providing food for his people. Although, bitter, Naomi's hope survived her grief. She knew God's character and trusted in God's provision. It was through her faith and trust in God that her daughter-in-law Ruth also trusted and believed. Ruth, also in her grief had confidence in the God that Naomi served.

"But those that wait for the Lord shall renew their strength, they shall mount up with wings like eagles, they shall run and not be weary, they shall walk and not faint."

Isaiah 40:31 (NRSV)

While You Wait

Hope in its seed form also carries patience and willingness to wait. Hope allows you to wait with anticipation of a good outcome. Our modern day, technological culture loathes waiting. We do not like waiting for food, so we choose fast food, drive through places over dine-in restaurants. We do not want to wait for food to cook on the stove so we place it in the microwave oven. However, there are some things that we are willing to wait for. There are some things in our individual lives that we deem is worth the wait. We wait for the special mate to marry. *(Hopefully.)* We wait for the ideal house to purchase. We wait in line to see our favorite musician or entertainer. We wait because we choose to wait. We have to do the same thing with hope.

While you are going through turmoil in your life you have to make the choice to hope. You have to decide that the promises of God are worth the wait. Make the choice to wait, while help for your situation is on the way. The healing you desire for your brokenness is in progress. The mending of your heart is going to take place. The pain from your situation will cease one day. Make hope your choice of medicine while dealing with the hurts of life. When you choose hope, you choose life and you choose God. Choose to live the abundant life that God has promised you while waiting for its full manifestation. Choose to remember God and be encouraged by God's faithfulness. Choose to hold on to promises instead of your fears.

When tragedy strikes, we long for the day that we no longer feel the hurt and disappointment of our life. When trauma devastates the life we lived as normal we have no immediate vision of how our life will ever be normal again. Day after day, we live with the pain, hurt and disappointment and question, "Where is God?" We soon realize that the length of our journey will be a hard one as we discover new terrain. This is when our life support system of hope kicks in. Hope anchors us and keeps us firm and secure while we are fighting for our lives.

If you somehow feel that you have been losing or even lost hope, understand that hope can be restored. All you have to do is make the choice as the first step. Look for God's hand during this journey and watch God restore your hope. Look for the small blessings along the way. Search for the small milestones and allow it to breathe life into your hope. Remember the promises of God and pray them daily. This is how you survive. This is how you live on hope until help arrives.

Once you understand how crucial hope is, you will live to protect it at all costs. You will treasure your hope and work to keep your "hope tank" full. We all need and desire to be hopeful and not hopeless. When you are full of hope, you are full of God. When you are full of God, nothing is impossible.

As you read this book, my prayer for you is echoed in the words of Paul.

"May the God of hope fill you with all the joy and peace as you trust in him, so that you may overflow with hope by the power of the Holy Spirit."

Romans 15:13 (NIV)

I believe that as you continue to put your hope in God, it will sustain you while you are in between seasons of the seed and fruit of faith.

❧ Journey Steps ❧

- **Confession**: In spite of my _____, (name tragedy, trauma, or loss) I choose to live on hope and remember the promises of God. I will pray the promises of God and not the problem. I will not give up my hope. I will keep my hope and faith in God.

- **Application**: Diagnose the symptoms of hopelessness as described in this chapter. Find the scriptures (promises of God) that speak to the particular condition and confess, meditate and pray on them.

- **Prayer Starter**: Dear God, when my hope feels like it is failing, renew my strength, joy and peace so that I may overflow with hope by the power of your holy spirit. Uproot all seeds of hope deferred and allow only faith to grow. Water it daily with your love and care so that I am always reminded of your faithfulness.

- **Scripture Meditation:** Psalm 62:5, Hebrews 6:19, 1 Peter 5:7, Romans 15:13, Isaiah 40:31

SECTION THREE

Your New Life

7

Reservations for Your New Season

"That person is like a tree planted by streams of water, which yields its fruit in season and whose leaf does not whither-- whatever they do prospers."

Psalm 1:3 (NIV)

One spring, I wanted to redesign my flower bed in front of my home. I wanted to plant annuals so each season I would be welcomed by flowers. In a store, I saw the beautiful tulips, which hadn't yet reached full bloom. I bought them and planted its bulbs because it was still cold outside, although we were hovering on the cusp of spring. Tulips are bulbs in its seed form and bulbs require the harsh winter cold to fully bloom in spring. To my disappointment most of the tulips didn't blossom. Unfortunately, I realized too late that I planted them in the wrong season.

> *"To everything there is a season, and a time to every purpose under the heaven."*
>
> *Ecclesiastes 3:1*

Ecclesiastes 3:1 - 8 reminds us that there is a time and season for everything. A season is a duration of time marked by certain characteristics. Winter, Spring, Summer and Fall are the earth's seasons which bear specific identifying characteristics. Each season has a purpose under heaven and is marked with a beginning and an end.

If you are reading this book, certainly you are familiar with cold, dark seasons. In this particular season, the pain never ceases and hurt never heals. You feel as if no one understands what you are going through. Feeling alone and abandoned you are living in a perpetual state of grief, unhappiness, anger and/or bitterness. In this season, it is constantly raining and the storms seem to never cease. Just when you think the sun might come out, it begins to rain some more. Now you have succumbed to your own reasoning that this storm will never end. Now is a good opportunity to remind you that a season is a duration of time, and not your lifetime.

God operates in seasons under the principles of seed, time and harvest. (Genesis 9:22) When you understand the Season that you are in, you stop looking for the clock and start looking for revelation. As you journey with grace through life, it is important to discern which season that you are in and identify its characteristics. Here are a few reasons why this is important to discern your season:

1. You can prepare yourself mentally, spiritually and physically to endure it, until your change comes.

2. It will provide you with a sense of peace and direction even if it is a dry or cold season.

3. You will better understand that the plan that God has for your life is to prosper you, give you hope and bring you to an expected end.

4. It will allow you to pray strategically and differently for the different seasons.

It is vital that you discern and embrace the season that you are in. If not, you will live in a state of frustration and disappointment. You cannot try to uproot in a season that is designated for planting. You cannot plant in a season designed for uprooting. If you are in a planting season, it may seem like all you are doing is giving and laboring without any reward.

"Let us not become weary in doing good, for at the proper time we will reap a harvest if we do not give up."

Galatians 6:9 (NIV)

Discerning Your Season

I was driving to pick up my son from his new school, in our new state. It was a drive I made daily for over a year at that point. Some days in tears, some days in distress, some days in fatigue and some days at peace like this day. As I pulled up to the small Christian school, God chose that moment to reveal to me a vision. I sat in suspense in the turning lane, waiting for a safe left turn. I glimpsed at the roof of the building and saw boxes just falling into place. In a very orderly fashion, the boxes were being selectively stacked and fitting snuggly into its precise location like a puzzle piece.

After safely making my left turn, I shifted the car into park and waited in the car for my son and to hear from God. Speaking in that soft, authoritative inner voice God explained to me that I was in a season of Order. In that season of Order, there were some things in my life that had to be properly placed in order, before that breakthrough or full restoration could take place. There were some things that God was working out, putting into place and there were some things that I had to do as well. God had to organize, people, places and opportunities for my next season.

Through that vision, I saw the hand of God working on my behalf, but within God's timing. Although, I wanted it to be my season of reaping and restoration, it was not yet time. I also knew I was not still in that cold, dark season of winter either. I was in my season that God called Order.

In this chapter, I want you to take the time to discern the season that God has you in currently. This requires prayer and being able to hear from God. During your private worship, enter into the presence of God and allow God to minister to your heart. If you have not yet reached a place in your prayer life or worship that you can hear the voice of God, now is the time to press. If you have never been so lost in worshiping God that you forget temporarily where you are, now is a good time to start. When you are worshipping God in Spirit and in truth, it gives you the most intimate audience with God. That is the most incredible place to be.

Once you have discerned that season, embrace it knowing that it is not a permanent place. Although this may sound elusive to some, it is not as difficult to achieve as one might think. As God shifts us in and out of seasons, God will give us a word. God sends dreams, visions or a prophetic messenger with a word especially for us that sustain us during the seasons.

Reservations for Your New Season

"For the jar of flour was not used up and the jug of oil did not run dry, in keeping with the word of the Lord spoken by Elijah."

1 Kings 17:16 (NIV)

Almost a year after my late husband died, my dreams began to intensify. I began having multiple dreams each and every night. I began writing them down and God led me to a book on how to interpret dreams. I understood a lot more about the importance of understanding your dreams. I was also able to discern which dreams were sent to torture my spirit, warn me of an impending danger or provide revelation in my life.

God will also send a prophet to speak into your life or provide you with prophetic revelation, just like the word sent to the Widow of Zarepath. Nowadays, many people including Christians do not understand nor receive personal prophecy. However, God still uses people to be God's voice in the earth.

When you receive personal prophecy correctly it will provide you with insight into the plan and purpose of God for your life. When you know the purpose of God, understand His will and bring yourself into alignment with that plan, a new birth takes place.

When I came to my new city and began attending Seminary, there was a fellow student whom I didn't know personally but we took a few classes together. Every time I would say hello to her she would just begin to speak to me with what seemed like randomness in the beginning.

However, as I listened more intently I realized she was pouring life into me through her words. Without fail, anytime I would walk into her presence, I would just let her talk and I wouldn't say a word. I got to the point of writing everything she said down and would re-read it at different times, meditate on it or when necessary pray about it. I was amazed months and even years later how affirming her words were to me. This is how you receive personal prophecy.

Prophecy is not just about foretelling future events, but it also clarifies your current situation as well. Dreams and visions have the same purpose and will reveal things to you that only God can. You may not like what you hear at times, but don't shoot the messenger. You may not like who the messenger is, but don't discredit the message. The message could be the one word that reveals God's intended will in your season. It could be the one word that will carry you through the crossroads of indecision and provision.

When you understand the season that you are in, you stop looking at the clock and start looking for revelation.

Crossroads

There were times during my distress when I was so angry with God for allowing my life to crumble although I would not verbally admit it. When the pain did not stop I said to myself, *"I give up."* I felt completely defeated by my circumstances and felt I couldn't do anything but give up. So I said it. *"I give up."* And then I waited. And waited. I'm not sure what I was waiting for exactly. The sky didn't go black. The earth didn't swallow me up in its belly. Nothing changed.

My circumstances didn't magically change for the better or worse because I "gave up." Then I just laughed at myself because I realized I didn't know what giving up meant. Was I going to give up my salvation? I already believed that Jesus is the Son of God and that He died for our sins and was resurrected. So that wasn't going to work. Was I going to stop serving God? Not when the only alternative was serving the devil?

It did not take me long to realize that giving up was not a practical option for me. I discovered that when giving up is not an option trusting God always prevails. Although, while giving up was not an option, living through it seemed insurmountable. However, it is in that single moment I realized that God is all that I had left.

Going back to life as normal after a tragedy, trauma or loss, doing simple things like going to the grocery store, picking up dry cleaning, or walking out your front door becomes very different and nothing about it feels normal. Actually, nothing in life feels normal. Life has changed and there is no going back to yesterday, last week, or even last month.

When tragedy strikes and your child is shot multiple times sitting in her first grade class, your heart feels like it was shot as well. When your husband goes to work at an accounting firm and a plane hits the building and it collapses, you feel like you are crumbling along with it. You find yourself on a roller coaster ride of sorrow, death and despair to which you either embrace God or turn your back. When you are knee deep in the middle of a crisis, you will find yourself between two mindsets. You wonder, *"Should I run or should I hide? Should I fight or should you take flight? Should I give up or should I trust God?"*

It is in these moments that time seems to temporarily stand still. It recognizes you have a paramount choice to make that determines the duration of your current season.

God will send you a word that will sustain you in between seasons.

The Moment of Truth

My life was held up in the balance for months, which made things extremely difficult for me financially and emotionally. I had no clue when my husband's body would be recovered from the icy river and when we would be able to put his body to rest. I had no other source of consistent income than my husband's and didn't know how I was going to feed my child, and keep a shelter over us. Creditors were ready to repossess our one good working car and our house was already in pre-foreclosure. I was the ostracized widow living under the stigma of suicide, with the whispers of what happened and uncertainty about my future. I couldn't even prove he had died and couldn't do a thing with life insurance or anything else. The most humbling experience from a dual degreed, entrepreneur was applying for food stamps.

At one point, I had placed my son in the care of family friends because I could not function for the both of us. I didn't like him seeing me cry so much or just lay in my bed with my long red robe. I lived in fear of the doorbell ringing and having to deal with the police officers and the news of finding my husband's body. The last thing I wanted was to have my son witness more police coming to the house and watching me handle more difficult news. Hearing the doorbell created such fear and anxiety to the point that my friends asked visitors to knock on the door or call before coming. The days turned into weeks, weeks into months and I realized I could no longer hold my breath. I had a moment of truth.

Living life on pause because you haven't returned to your normal life is like a child who holds their breath until they get their way. I had three choices. Either I continue to hold my breath and pass out due to the lack of oxygen to the brain. Or, continue to cry in the hopes that God would feel sorry for me and do what I need Him to do when I need Him to do it. The only remaining option would be to breathe again and begin living again. I chose the latter, mainly for the life of my son. I had to live because he had to live. This was my moment of truth, therefore, I took off the long red robe and I decided to live. My heart echoed these words:

"I shall not die, but live, and declare the works of the Lord."

Psalm 118:17 (KJV)

When you realize that the trash has to go out, you have to take a shower, you have to eat and the kids have to go to school -- that is your moment of truth. When you decide to breathe because you realize you didn't die -- that is your moment of truth. When your child is gone and you accept that they are with God – that is your moment of truth. You experience a moment of truth when you realize that you have to begin living again and you do it! What do you need to take off in this season in order to live again? Have you experienced your moment of truth?

Once you can accept that the life that you had no longer exists, you have to determine what changes you need to make in order to accommodate your new life. You may need to change you work hours or job to accommodate being a new single parent. You may need to discard all materials left over from an abusive relationship. You now have the opportunity to have a fresh start in life.

When life beats you into the muck and myrrh in the valley of sorrow, you become immune to the plan God has for your life. Your vision is clouded by your tears. When you are held hostage to your memories of yesterday, they disenable you from making new memories today. For most of us, we won't ever return to an old life and just fall back in step with everyone else. Our lives have changed forever and we have to walk in a new life with a new beginning. I dare you today to make a choice.

- ☑ Choose life
- ☑ Chose joy
- ☑ Choose courage
- ☑ Choose boldness
- ☑ Choose change
- ☑ Choose forgiveness
- ☑ Choose the present
- ☑ Choose hope
- ☑ Choose God
- ☑ Choose love

When you make a choice to live this abundant life fully, you are actually making reservations to your new season. You might not be there yet, but your new season will arrive.

Own Your Kairós

Have you ever felt like the clock continues to tick with no change in sight? Days turn into weeks, weeks roll into months, and months painfully into years. The calendar continues year after year. Unfortunately, it is not moved by our tears, pain or distress. The Greek language has two words for time – chronos and kairos. Chronos is chronological time and deals with time as recorded by a clock and calendar. When you were born, the time and date was recorded with chronos.

Kairós means opportune time. It is derived from the word *kara* which means "head," referring to things, "coming to a head." It is the opportune time to take full advantage. Kairós has little to do with chronological time and everything to do with suitable time, the moment of opportunity and the appointed time for God to fulfill His purpose. As a matter of fact, kairós can be defined as pregnant time.

When Naomi left Moab to return home to Bethlehem, she left bitter, hurt and empty. However, when she made the choice to leave, she made the choice to live again. When she made that choice, she unknowingly made a reservation to her new season. She traveled to Bethlehem grudgingly with her daughter-in-law Ruth that was also widowed. When the women arrived in Bethlehem, they arrived to a new barley season.

Barley was a major food, especially among the poor as well as a crop for animals. Barley is the first to harvest in the spring, and then followed by wheat. Naomi and Ruth arrived at just the right time to obtain food and store some for the winter. When the harvesters cut the sheaves, a remnant would remain on the ground to which gleaners follow behind them and pick it up. Hebrew law required that anything that fell would remain for the poor and often women would glean.

Ruth went to the fields, at the approval of Naomi to glean in a particular field. The field just happened to belong to Boaz, who was the family of Naomi's husband Elimelek. Ruth found favor in Boaz's fields. Boaz allowed her to glean as much as she wanted under his protection and care. Ruth gleaned through the barley and wheat season making provisions for both her and her mother-in-law. This was just the beginning of the plan that God had for their lives.

Their arrival was the start of their new season. In this new season, they were met with an opportunity for God's appointed time to fulfill His purpose – Kairós. They did not arrive to Boaz's field by accident. Since Boaz was kin to Elimelek he was Naomi's kinsman-redeemer. This was a legal term for someone that had an obligation to redeem a relative in serious difficulty. Naomi still owned her husband's land, to which Boaz bought and took ownership of it, but also married Ruth. Ruth and Boaz had a son, to which they named Obed. Obed, was the father of Jesse, and Jesse was the father of David. When you follow the genealogy of David throughout the scriptures it will lead you to Jesus, our Lord and Savior.

Naomi took care of the child and it became the turnaround in Naomi's life. She was restored fully. She was no longer a stranger in a strange land, with no male provider. She had family, new life and purpose. Naomi and Ruth were presented with the right opportunity at the right time. It was all a part of God's bigger plan of redemption.

Even through the tragedy, trauma and loss, God still has a plan. Becoming childless, widowed, divorced or victimized will not end your world, but it will propel you into a new one. There is a wonderful new world waiting for you. There is life after death, happiness after divorce and wholeness after brokenness. Although, you may be in the cold, dark season of uncertainty it will not last forever. Learn from the season that you are in and God's healing process to take root in your life. Make a choice in your life today that you shall live and declare the works of the Lord. Make that reservation for your new season and watch God reveal to you the bigger plan for your life.

❧ Journey Steps ☙

- ***Confession:*** I declare that in this season I will become stronger and wiser. I shall not give up. I shall live and declare the works of the Lord. I will trust the plan that God has for my life.

- ***Application:*** Discern your current season through prayer, worship and prophetic revelation. Identify your moment of truth. Make a to-do-list of things you can adjust to accommodate your "new normal."

- ***Prayer Starter:*** Dear God, my heart and my soul hopes in you. Grant me understanding of my season that I might learn from it. Help me to make the right decision during the crossroads of my life.

- ***Scripture Meditation:*** Philippians 2:6, 1 Kings 17:16, Psalm 104:27, Galatians 6:9, Matthew 7:7

8

New Purpose on the Other Side of Pain

"Being confident of this very thing, that He who has begun a good work in you will complete it until the day of Jesus Christ."

Philippians 1:6 (NKJV)

The sounds of worship music penetrated the airwaves as I sat on the pew of my church. Like most Sundays, the atmosphere shifted into a loud praise and everyone around me began clapping, singing and dancing for the Lord. However, there was something stirring in my spirit which caused me just to sit still and discern what was happening. Then God began speaking and ministering to my heart regarding the call on my life. I heard that call seventeen years prior, but ran as far away from it as I could. God did not stop calling nor using me, however, this was a different ring tone. God began explaining the ministry God was calling out of me: teaching, preaching and prophesy. Just as a daddy talks to his daughter, God spoke soft enough for me not to feel overwhelmed but stern enough that I would finally listen.

For the first time after 15 years of God calling, finally a yes rang out in my spirit and in my will. I said yes to God. I bowed before God to the point that it brought me to my knees. I wept holding my stomach that was filling up with hope and expectation. I whispered yes until it rang in my soul and rooted in my will. I didn't know how or what it would require me to do, but I knew the first step was me saying yes. Six months later, I woke up to the assassination plot on my life, family, ministry and purpose. I had no clue that saying yes would result in a pain in my life that was this unimaginable. However, there was promise attached to my purpose and my pain.

God keeps His promises

For centuries her story has been retold. Practically everyone in the world has heard at least something about her. Like most girls, she was young when she became engaged through an arranged marriage. She was simply a young, Jewish girl living a pretty ordinary life, with ordinary circumstances, in an ordinary town. Nothing really spectacular happened there. It was a small isolated town with a population of about 200 people. That small town of Nazareth in Galilee along with all other Jews of the day were awaiting the Messiah, the Savior that God promised would fulfill all promises.

God promised Abraham that his descendants would be a great nation and God would be their God forever. God promised David that salvation would come through his lineage. For centuries, their ancestors waited on the promised Messiah.

I believe that she often wondered if her life really mattered. The glass ceiling for a woman in a patriarchal culture was to be a wife, mother or more realistically to give a man a legitimate heir. That was the goal for every young girl. Imagine young Mary's surprise when she received the visit from the angel Gabriel. First he shows up unannounced - no call, email, or text message. Then addresses her as "highly favored one," and informs her that the Lord is with her.

Naturally, this angelic visitation struck fear all through her as it would any of us. However, the visitation wasn't even the most incredible thing that happened that day. It was the message that Gabriel brought that would change her life forever. Gabriel said,

"Mary, you have found favor with God. And now you will conceive in your womb and bear a son, and you will name him Jesus. He will be great, and will be called Son of the Most High, and the Lord God will give to him the throne of his ancestor David. He will reign over the house of Jacob forever, and of his kingdom there will be no end."

Luke 1:30-33 (NRSV)

This was the most exciting, albeit confusing, news Mary had ever received. There were two wonderful things that were about to take place. First, the long waited Messiah that would give them hope through the hardship of Roman rule was about to be born. This Messiah would give a voice to the voiceless and power to the powerless.

This astounding news meant that not only the past promises would be fulfilled, but the future was limitless with God. For nothing *will* be impossible with God. That is a promise in the future tense. Therefore, God is saying, *'Not only will I keep the promises I've made in the past, but I'm going to make some new promises and keep those too.'* This was the moment that Mary and the rest of us learned, that God keeps His promises. It doesn't matter who God has to use, God keeps His promises. No matter how impossible the circumstances are God still keeps His promises. God will keep His promises concerning you as well.

The Word of God is full of promises to those that believe. God has a long, proven track record of being a promise keeper. God established covenant with us from the beginning of time. Even when we mess up, doubt God or even walk away from God, the covenant is still intact. The covenant God makes is inclusive of a grace and mercy policy that covers us in times of crisis and neglect.

Throughout their often rocky relationship with God, the children of Israel were always reminded of the promises of God. Even when they were being punished. As a matter of fact, the children of Israel were in exile when God used Jeremiah to comfort them with these words:

"For I know the plans that I have for you," declares the lord, "plans to prosper you and not to harm you, plans to give you hope and a future. Then you will seek me and find me when you seek me with all your heart. I will be found by you," declares the Lord, "and will bring you back from captivity. I will gather you from all the nations and places where I have banished you," declares the Lord, "and will bring you back to the place from which I carried you into exile."

Jeremiah 29:11-14(NIV)

If God can keep His promises when we are at fault, surely God can keep His promises when we are suffering through no fault of our own. It is important to remember that God has a plan for our lives and even a plan for the pain. There is not a hurt, pain, or trouble that you endure that God will ever waste. It is through crisis situations do we have to remember the promises of God and pray them daily, as it will encourage a downtrodden soul. You have to pray the promise and not the problem because God responds to God's Word.

When you are traveling on this journey back to the land of the living, you must hold onto the promises of God. God enjoys that. God takes pleasure in you holding on to what God promised. It takes faith to hold on, and faith is what pleases God.

God has a plan for the pain in your life.

Your Purpose is a part of God's Plan
The second thing that excited Mary in this angelic message was that the Messiah would be born through her. Imagine every young Jewish girl who had been wondering and hoping that she might be the one chosen for this great honor. Nonetheless, it was Mary, the poor, ordinary young woman from Nazareth, whom God favored. Who wouldn't want God's favor? Everybody wants God's favor. We want favor on the job, favor in the world, favor with our debts and favor for our children. Consequently, for Mary, favor was getting pregnant, out of wedlock by the Holy Spirit, while engaged to a carpenter.

Mary's favor jeopardized her entire ordinary and humble life. If Joseph didn't marry her she could have remained unmarried for life. If her father had rejected her too she could have been forced into a life of begging or prostitution.

Mary discovered that favor is scandalous, controversial and even painful. Mary's incredible story brought shame to herself and her family. Of course, shame brings pain, rejection and often abandonment. However, God had a master plan that included Mary and her pain, scorn and everything else.

Mary accepted the plan and gave herself up wholly to do God's will. Her assignment and purpose for her life was clear at that point. Additionally, she saw the plan of God and her role in it. In order to fulfill the old promises and establish the new promises, God had to come and do it Himself. As a result, God, the giver of life, connected with a receiver of life, so that God can enter humanity and give us all eternal life.

While it wasn't easy living out the uncertainties and pain of her assignment, the one thing that kept her going she knew that she was giving birth to hope for her people and ultimately humanity.

Every child of God has a purpose to which we are given an assignment. Our purpose and assignment does not change because our life changes after crisis. In fact, often it is the tragedy, trauma and loss that define that purpose for us. What is your assignment in the earth? Everybody has one. What has God purposed and called you to do? The mark of the Redeemed or Christian is that we live out of the knowledge of God that has been given to us. God has endowed each of us with gifts beyond measure.

Regardless of everything that you are going through, God still has a plan and purpose for your life. God created you with special gifts and passions, ultimately to serve others. It is imperative that we live our lives on purpose or else we lose sight of what really matters in our lives. Even if you have been detoured in life, God's purpose for your life has not changed.

Through crisis, we may forget about the plan that God has on our life. If you were involved in ministry, serving in your local church, missions, etc., you may be discouraged or perhaps hurt by the fact that such circumstances have happened to you. Even more, you might have stopped attending church, resigned your position or even abandoned your ministry. While sabbaticals are permissive, resignation and abandonment is not.

When I felt the most useless, God said that I would teach, preach and speak prophetically again. You will return to being used by God. You shall sing again. You shall preach again. You shall teach again. You shall speak in His name again. I declare and decree right now in the name of Jesus that you will serve in the Kingdom of God all the days of your life. Your life is a part of God's master plan. When you were born, God had a unique purpose for you and God desires that you live out that purpose daily *and* in spite of your pain.

Your Destiny is Greater than Your Pain.

"While they were there, the time came for her to deliver her child. And she gave birth to her firstborn son and wrapped him in bands in cloth, and laid him in a manger, because there was no place for them in the inn."

Luke 2:6-7 (NRSV)

Like any other birth, the pain was a part of the process. And YES, it was painful. The angel said Mary would *conceive* supernaturally, not *give birth* supernaturally.

I'm pretty sure she felt the pain and it was real. There was no epidural, anesthesia, Vicodin or any other drugs to escape the pain. Like Mary, I endured two out of three of my children's births without an epidural. The first contractions weren't as painful as I imagined. I thought to myself, I can do this. I don't know what women complain about, it hurts but it's tolerable. Then the contractions got closer, more painful and less tolerable.

In my imagination I can see Mary in the same predicament with the same kind of pain. She was probably wishing she had her momma with her instead of 80 miles away in Nazareth. Now, she is reminded that she was a stranger in Bethlehem, having her first child out of wedlock. She is lying on the ground, hay in her hair with smelly animals all around her staring. They were probably wondering why she was not in Bethlehem Memorial Hospital in a birthing suite.

In the midst of all that pain, something changes and it is no longer just the pain of the contractions. Physically, labor pain is the tightening of the uterus, which opens up the cervix. The cervix stays closed during pregnancy, but the contractions allow it to open so that birth can take place. The stronger the contraction, the easier it is for the cervix to open. When women are giving birth, the pain is not welcomed but that open cervix is welcomed and needed. The pain serves a purpose. Imagine that? Imagine there being a purpose to the pain that you have experienced. Imagine the Creator of our bodies knew how to purpose pain in order to bring forth new life.

Eventually, the pain of the contractions creates an incredible pressure inside of a laboring woman. The pressure is not painful, but it is the ultimate indicator that the baby had descended down the birth canal and its head is right on the edge. Some of you may be at this exact same point, right on the edge of new life.

You have been through the pain of your circumstances. Now you feel the extreme pressure on every side. You are right on the edge of your destiny being fulfilled. You are right on the edge of all promises being fulfilled. You are right on the edge of your break through but the pain is real. Nevertheless, we have to remember that pain is temporary. Pain or trouble does not last. So do not make permanent decisions based on a temporary pain. Don't give up in the pain. Don't turn back now. There is a greater purpose for your pain. Your destiny is greater than your pain.

Mary, the mother of our Lord, could not give up because there was a greater purpose for her pain. She wasn't just carrying a child, but was also carrying someone else's destiny – Jesus. And He was not only carrying His destiny, but He was carrying everybody else's destiny too. There was a greater purpose on the other side of her pain. I know that it has been a rough journey, but you have to push through the pain to get to the other side of your purpose.

You have to make the decision in the midst of the hurt, pain and disappointment you can't stay in that place called There. There is joy on the other side of this pain. There is peace on the other side of this situation. There is a destiny on the other side of tragedy. There is life after death. There is love after divorce. There are blessings on the other side of the trauma that happened to you. However, to get to the other side you have to push through the pain.

Mary pushed through the pain that day and gave birth to her son. But she also gave birth to her destiny, her son's destiny and everybody's destiny. God entered humanity as a humble baby, from a poor, little Jewish girl. Mary walked in her purpose, and she fulfilled her destiny. Then, Jesus had to fulfill his own destiny for his life. Now, it is your turn. Your outlook on this journey depends on your faith. Your faith decides your future.

When I was hanging onto life and felt death approaching, God didn't show me my past. God showed me my future.

There was nothing in my past that needed me. There was nothing in my past that I could change. There is no life in the past and if you try to live in the past it will suffocate you. God showed me my future to refocus the trajectory of my life after death. While God was with me in the valley of the shadow of death, God pulled down the big screen TV so I could see the purpose of my life. I realized that my life was not over, instead it was just beginning. I discovered purpose on the other side of pain and I believe you can too.

You have to fulfill your destiny, in spite of it all. Your future is filled with your destiny. Every promise that God wrote in His Word, spoke in your heart and prophesied to you, God will perform. It is God's desire that you fulfill your destiny and will use the pains of life to prepare you for your purpose and for your victory.

❧ Journey Steps ❧

- *Confession*: I will push through the pain to get to the other side of my destiny.

- *Application*: Develop a vision board for your life. Include areas of ministry. Pray and ask God for favor, wisdom and strategy for accomplishing the board.

- *Prayer Starter*: Dear God, I confess this has been the most painful time in my life. However, I believe that all of it will not be wasted. God, I trust the plan that you have for my life. I will push through the pain and allow you to bring me to my expected end. I will hold on to every promise you have spoken to me and written in your Word.

- *Scripture Meditation*: Jeremiah 33:2, Titus 1:2-3, Jeremiah 29:11, 2 Corinthians 1:20-22

9

The Victory Lap

"You enlarged my path under me, so my feet did not slip."

Psalm 18:36 (NKJV)

Sluggishly running down the block I felt like my legs were turning into a pile of spaghetti and my limp body was about to be on the ground if I didn't stop at that exact moment. I was so disappointed with myself because I couldn't make it around the block or even to the corner. I had no other choice but to simply walk. Although I wasn't able to run like I hoped, I was able to get the same mileage by walking.

However, a few years later, I eventually replaced my disappointment with excitement as I discovered an unsuspecting place of breakthrough and restoration for me. My love for outdoor recreation and need for solace was found in my local park. Beautiful lakes surround the jogging trail with the cutest ducks sitting on the banks or wading in the water. Nature is my place of solitude, comfort and peace so I typically get to the park early before too many people are on the trail.

That is where I am welcomed by the quacks and swim strokes of the ducks that cheer for me as I hustle by them. As the temperature rises and the sun becomes hot, the majestic, aged trees tower over me and cool me with its shadow and gentle breeze. The hues of the beautiful rose bushes always make me smile and feel just as beautiful. This is my place of refuge from the noise of the world and the noise in my head. When I am there, my mind is clear and open to receive. This is where God downloads me, encourages and whispers to me through the wind as it brushes my cheeks.

One day on a typical walk, I found my mind hurdling through all the things that I had been going through. My heart began to race, my legs started to feel lighter and I felt the urge to run. I started to jog quickly and then I thought to myself I had better slow down before I fall. Suddenly, I found a stride that matched my heart's rhythm and I continued to run. Surprisingly, I did not fall. I did not get winded. I continued to run.

As I ran, I glimpsed over my shoulder and saw how far I ran without stopping. I heard the ducks saying to each other, *"I knew she could do it."* Encouraged, I smiled and continued running as long and as far as my breathing and my legs would allow me to go. Then, I started thinking about everything that happened to me. I remembered all the pain I had endured but God's grace kept me in the race. My heart exploded with such gratitude and a victorious spirit filled my soul. I began to run as fast and as hard as I could, then I just broke down and cried. I had been through some dark places, but I made it out alive and well. I had been in that place called There, but now I was walking in the land of the living and thriving.

Thriving After Surviving

All of us who endure tragedy, trauma and loss will eventually realize what we have survived and celebrate. However, there are many people that will remain in survival mode. In that mode, defensive and safety mechanisms are high. You may find yourself mistrusting and self-isolated. It is necessary to transition from survival mode to thriving mode. In this transition you are not just surviving what happened to you but you are thriving, growing and prospering. This is the time where you re-define your bliss and maintain your peace.

When I counsel people who are in this transition, I always ask them, *"What makes you happy?"* After they nervously smile and answer, I respond with, *"Pursue that."* Walking outdoors makes me happy. When I am stressed or just need an audience with God, I go for a walk in my park. It has become my sanctuary and now a spiritual practice. That is what I pursue.

This is the phase in your journey where you have to become intentional with your spiritual well-being. This is the time where you find the good moments in all of the bad that has happened to you and multiply them. It is okay to buy yourself flowers if you love them. It is perfectly normal to redecorate your bedroom and give it a fresh look. It is quite acceptable to change hair styles and experiment with new colors. This is the best time to re-make something new, fresh and exciting. You do not have to try and fit back into your old life after tragedy, trauma or loss. God will give you a new life to fit into and it is a life that you can be at peace and happy.

"Finally, brothers and sisters, whatever is true, whatever is noble, whatever is right, whatever is pure, whatever is

The Victory Lap

lovely, whatever is admirable – if anything is excellent or praiseworthy – think about such things."

Philippians 4:9 (NRSV)

What gives you peace? Think on it! Is it your children? Is it your family? Is it God? That is what you should think about when your mind begins to unravel with thoughts about what happened. You should have a safe room in your mind filled with peace and praise that you can retreat to in stressing times. I discovered that when I entered a season of peace in my life that I had to fight to maintain it. There were people and conversations that I just could not engage myself in. There were warfare prayers I had to pray when anything threatened my peace. When you had to travel a long hard journey to achieve peace, you will fight to keep it at all costs. Seek peace and pursue it and run this race with perseverance.

The Land of the Living

Every athlete has to train hard, make sacrifices and expend enormous amounts of energy into their sport in order to excel. When a track athlete runs a race and wins, their excitement is uncontainable. Their exuberance is a result of every ache and pain they endured along the way. When they cross that finish line they also cross the threshold of their manifested dreams. It is at this point that they realize that which they suffered through was worth it all.

After you have journeyed from death to life and brokenness to wholeness, you obtain a new stride. You become stronger, wiser and finally feel the victory that you already had. As a child of God, by default you are an overcomer. There is a great victorious feeling when you realize that you have fought the fight and won. Now you are ready to take flight and run your victory laps like a triumphant athlete.

A Ugandan hurdler by the name of John Akii-Bua was the first Olympic winner from Uganda. At the Munich Olympics of 1972, John Akii-Bua won the gold medal after clearing the 400 meter hurdles in 47.82 seconds, setting an astonishing new world record. After winning the gold medal, he was so overwhelmed with joy that when a spectator handed him a Ugandan flag, he ran around the track with the flag in what is considered the first victory lap. Running a victory lap has become a very familiar sight as it has become a tradition in track and in motorsports. However, victory laps are not just for athletes and race car drivers.

When you have re-entered the land of the living you have discovered your purpose and find strength through fulfilling it. The heart is full of gratitude, which fuels its obligations to others. When you are able to testify to what God has done for you, it is just like running a victory lap. Psalm 107:2 says,

"Let the redeemed of the Lord say so – whom He has redeemed from the hand of the enemy."

Psalm 107:2 (NKJV)

When you "say so" you are running your victory lap and giving God the glory He deserves. You are testifying of God's goodness. This is what it truly means to live in the land of the living. When you are living that victorious life you can proudly uphold the banner of God. The banner of God declares that it is God that made you victorious. You will praise, worship, bless and thank God for all that God has done for you during your valley experience.

As you travel on your journey, with God's grace and enter the land of the living, you are declaring you won. You were broken, but now you are whole. You may have been abused, but are no longer a victim.

People may have walked out on you, but you have walked into your destiny. You have walked into your new life. You have walked back into the land of the living. However, I wouldn't be a good tour guide if I let you walk in and walk away. The journey is not over yet.

The Truth about Victory

When you find yourself on the hardest and longest journey of your life, God will send people in your life that have traveled that road before you in order to encourage you with their experience and knowledge. While you are praising and blessing God for what He has done for you, do not forget those who are not yet running and still in their place called 'There.' A true sportsman won't run his victory lap alone. When you have been a recipient of that same encouragement, you pass it along with your newfound knowledge and wisdom. Your victory through your dark situation is another person's window to the light at the end of their tunnel.

In your victory lap you have a responsibility to grab someone's hand that has not yet finished the race. There will always be someone who will still be in the valley needing encouragement and direction. You will need to be that someone to hold their hand and let them know that there is life on the other side of their dark and hopeless situation. When you make it back to the land of the living, you can bear witness that there is life after death, healing after hurt, and love after betrayal. Once you have experienced the warmth of the light at the end of the tunnel you can testify that there is peace after the storm, acceptance after rejection, and wholeness after abandonment.

It can be very easy to fight your way to the top of the mountain of debris that used to be your life and stay there and celebrate your victory all day long. However, the very location of your victory enables you to look back and see where you have traveled from. In doing so, you will see others who are still in the hurting caravan of the woes of life. We owe it to God and to ourselves to help someone else along the way. It is not the will of God for us to have made it into our land of the living and not help our fellow brother and sister.

In the book of Numbers, when the children of Israel were ready to possess the land that God promised them, there were two and a half tribes whose inheritance was not on the other side of the Jordan River. Therefore, Moses commanded them to cross over the river with the other tribes and war with them until they have rest and are able to possess their land.

The Reubenites, the Gadites and the half tribe of Manasseh were obedient and helped the other tribes fight for their land and they were able to return to their land and enjoy it. This is how we show and operate in the love of God. This is how we demonstrate our victory and share it with others.

God does not bring us through something for us to share it with the worms under a dark rock. During the process of writing this book, people who had been watching me on my journey would contact me and ask how I made it through or let me know how encouraged they have been by my journey. When I used to think about all that I had been through, tears would often roll off my cheek and I would tell the Lord that I have to help other people so my journey would have been worth the hardship. Prior to the bottom of my life collapsing underneath me I was a very private person. Many of my friends and family didn't know of my trials in life until after I came through it and was bold enough to talk about it. Sharing the most devastating and intimate details of my life is extremely uncomfortable and humbling. I would have rather hid under a rock than discuss the most painful, embarrassing details of my life.

However, God constantly reminds me that the purpose of my writing was designed to 'heal, deliver and set the captives free." Every time I wanted to keep certain details out, God's voice would ring in my ears, *"I've come to set the captives free."* When I receive emails and calls from those captives who have been touched by my journey, I feel like that Olympic athlete jogging around the track doing a victory lap.

With all the billions of people on this planet, we are never truly alone. Even on the darkest paths and roads we take in life, we will come across persons along the journey in the same town of despair but just at a different address. When I was able to encourage the neighbors in my town of despair, my dry bones began to rattle.

Just two months into my ordeal I came across another young widow that I didn't know personally but when I heard about her tragic story through mutual Facebook friends. I reached out to her with whatever words of encouragement I had within me. I didn't have much to say, but I reached out my hand in the dark so that she knew there was someone else that understood her pain.

Then, it wasn't long after that I reconnected with a former co-worker who was going through a very dramatic and painful separation from his wife after his adulterous affair and legal woes. At that time we were both dealing with a treacherous amount of rejection and ironically bonded. However, as we were both wallowing in the woes of life I began to encourage him. The more I encouraged him, my heart was encouraged. The more encouragement I gave, the more my grief lifted. As my grief and pain lifted, my praise increased. My praise increased, not because my grief lifted, but because I was being used by God and my pain was not in vain.

God is a finisher.
God will complete the wok He began.

The Victory of Restoration

"But may the God of all grace, who called us to His eternal glory by Christ Jesus, after you have suffered a while, perfect, establish, strengthen and settle you."

1 Peter 5:10

When you purchase a house, you are required to purchase homeowner's insurance before you can close on the house. Homeowner's insurance will replace property from damage or theft and will even rebuild the entire home in the event of complete devastation. The only thing required from the policyholder is making the small monthly payments in obedience. Once you have done this and a claim is filed, everything that you lost is covered. Your faithfulness to God is your insurance policy. You can have peace knowing that as a child of God everything that you lost is covered and you will be restored.

"And I will restore to you the years that the locust hath eaten, the cankerworm, and the caterpillar, and the palmerworm, my great army which I sent among you."

Joel 2:25

God will restore everything you lost. Restoration is a part of victorious living. When you are restored, you are restored to God. You are made whole and usable for the Kingdom of God. God will restore your strength. God will restore your joy. God will restore your peace.

Sometimes restoration includes things and people. I can't promise that you will get everything you want, but I know God will give you everything that you need. Job lost all his children, property and servants but when he prayed for his friends, he received a double portion of all that he lost. Naomi lost her husband and her sons, she received a grandchild that was credited to her and all her needs were met, although she herself hadn't remarried. Ruth lost her husband, but remarried, and had a child that was in the lineage of Jesus. It is important to note here that not all things and people will return. However, you can still be restored, healed and made whole.

Victory does not come after everything in your life has been made perfect. It comes when you are able to stand in the midst of a broken life and recognize you are no longer broken. Despite being a 35-year old widow, single mother living in an unknown city separated or estranged from family and friends – I was victorious. Despite being talked about, criticized and ostracized – I was victorious. I still lived with the stigma and hardship of being a survivor of suicide. I still had to handle my son's questions regarding his father's death. Constantly, I was reminded of my widow status when filling out forms, fielding calls from creditors and meeting strangers who always asked how my husband died. However, when God restored my soul, gave me peace and healed my wounds, I walked in my victory.

God did not simply put back the pieces of my life, but painted me a new picture. God has given my life a new purpose, a new beginning and a new future. He has reversed the trajectory of my life and placed my feet onto a path of life, love and restoration. God blessed me with a wonderful new husband who is a loving father of our three children. God brought me back into the land of the living and He will bring you back too.

As you journey through this process of brokenness, hurt and pain, eventually your good days will outnumber your bad days. Your up days will overwhelm your down days. The darkness of the tunnel will seem to get brighter with each painful step, and you will sense daybreak approaching. Your sadness will peel away from your heart like a ripe, yellow banana and the oil of gladness will seep through the veins of your redeemed blood. You will be able to testify that God's grace truly is sufficient.

Grace for the Journey

"And the God of all grace, who called you to his eternal glory in Christ, after you have suffered in a little while, will himself restore you and make you strong, firm and steadfast."

I Peter 5:10 (NIV)

The journey back to the land of the living, as hard as it is, is not done alone. The grace of God is the powerful presence on the journey. Grace is the divine power that God gives His children that enables us to do what God has called us to do and be. This is the same power that is used to perform signs and wonders. (Acts 6:8) It is the same power that is made perfect in weakness. (2 Corinthians 12:9) The power of God is the grace of God which is accompanying you through this painful journey. God's power is being made perfect through your pain. It is through God's grace that you will be restored, made strong and steadfast.

Grace is the enabling power that keeps you walking in spite of the pain. Grace enables us to journey through that place called There while defeating weapons of mass torture. It is in the shadows of death where grace is found strategically navigating you around your destiny detours along the road to your comeback. God's grace sustains you in between hope and help as you await your new season. It is the strength that enables you to pursue your purpose on the other side of your pain as you run your victory lap.

In the midst of your tragedy, trauma and loss, you have all the grace and the power of God with you as you navigate back to the land of the living. Walk toward the light and remember God has given you grace for your journey.

Journey Steps

Confession: I am more than a Conqueror. I am an Overcomer. I am victorious. I can do all things through the power of God that is in me.

Application: Pray about someone who you can encourage by your story, then share it with them.

Prayer Starter: Dear God, Thank you for being with me along this journey. Thank you for never leaving me. I will praise and serve you for the rest of my days. I will hold up your banner and testify of your goodness. Thank you for blessing me with your power and your grace and accompanying me back to the land of the living.

Scripture Meditation: 2 Corinthians 12:9, 1 Corinthians 1:3-4

Notes

Chapter 1: That Place Called There

    1. http://www.apa.org/topic/trauma/

Chapter 6: Living on Hope until Help Arrives

    2. Dutch Sheets, The Power of Hope (Lake Mary, FL: Charisma House, 2014), Used by permission

Connect

Connect with the author and share your testimony about the help you received from this book. Your prayer requests are also welcome.

Athena C. Shack
Watersprings Media House
7095 Hacks Cross Road, #129
Olive Branch, MS 38654
www.grace4journey.com

Facebook: Grace for the Journey
Twitter: @grace4journey
Blog: www.grace4journey.com
Use #grace4journey

www.ingramcontent.com/pod-product-compliance
Lightning Source LLC
Chambersburg PA
CBHW072051290426
44110CB00014B/1631